HOW JUST
IS THE
WAR ON TERROR?

A Question of Morality

EILEEN P. FLYNN

Paulist Press
New York/Mahwah, NJ

Cover design by Joy Taylor
Book design by Lynn Else

Library of Congress Cataloging-in-Publication Data

Flynn, Eileen P. (Eileen Patricia)
    How just is the war on terror? : a question of morality / Eileen P. Flynn.
    p. cm.
    Includes bibliographical references and index.
    ISBN-13: 978-0-8091-4509-6 (alk. paper)
    1. Just war doctrine. 2. War—Religious aspects—Christianity. 3. War—Moral and ethical aspects. 4. Terrorism—Religious aspects—Christianity. 5. Terrorism—Moral and ethical aspects. I. Title.
    BT736.2.F597 2007
    172'.42—dc22

                                                                    2007020238

Published by Paulist Press
997 Macarthur Boulevard
Mahwah, New Jersey 07430

www.paulistpress.com

Printed and bound in the
United States of America

CONTENTS

To
Takako, Rick, and Janet

INTRODUCTION

It is simplistic to say that people learn ethics as children and that they somehow absorb an understanding about right and wrong that enables them to behave well or poorly as adolescents or adults. This is not to say that individuals do not assimilate attitudes and values during their formative years or that the do's and don'ts they are taught are unimportant. It is rather to assert that many of the ethical dilemmas people confront are very complex and that their resolution requires sophisticated analysis.

A new imperative was formulated a few years ago and we hear it referred to frequently: September 11, 2001, changed everything. Unpacking this slogan reveals that terrorists present a frightening threat to civilian populations and that communities that are threatened need to do all in their power to protect themselves. Of course, this is true, but it is also true that the traditional rules governing the use of military force have not changed, and these rules limit the actions that can be taken in counteracting terrorism.

The coordinated al-Qaeda attacks in the United States of September 11, 2001, followed by terrorist strikes in other places, including Madrid, Spain, on March 11, 2004, and London, England, on July 7, 2005,[1] forced governments to take action. Political leaders devised a two-pronged response. Searching for terrorists throughout the world and disbanding terrorist networks and training camps became the number one priority. Confronting nations that engage in terrorism or support terrorists also became a major objective.

Terrorism Raises New Questions

The events of 9/11 in New York City and Washington, D.C., ushered in a new reality. The devastating attacks on the United

States by foreign terrorists who wanted to harm our nation because they disagreed with our government's policies or our way of life[2] shattered the sense of security that had characterized the nation before September 11, 2001. Approximately three thousand people were killed on 9/11; men, women, and children of every religion and of none, and of innumerable ethnicities, lost their lives.

Once the initial shock that followed the attacks wore off, U.S. government leaders began to formulate a response. The 9/11 attackers made people realize that we could no longer come and go as though we were safe and had nothing to worry about; we needed to take action to thwart future terrorist attacks. Our leaders found themselves in uncharted waters because the war on terrorism that the nation undertook differed from any other war that our leadership had ever prosecuted.

Principles for deciding about going to war and for guiding combat in war are well established and are addressed in chapter 1 of this book. But applying the principles post–9/11 requires prudential judgments. These judgments, or decisions about what actions to take to guard against terrorism, are made by civilian and military leaders and are communicated to the personnel who conduct the so-called war on terror.

Women and men who join the military make a significant transition as they change from civilian to military status. Their training emphasizes physical fitness, instruction in combat skills, and learning focused on the particular tasks they will be assigned to perform. In addition, recruits learn to obey their commanders, and they come to understand how the chain of command functions in the military. To the extent that it is possible, those who join the military services also receive psychological preparation so that they can prepare themselves to withstand the stresses and horrors they may face in the course of active duty.

The aspect of preparation that this book focuses on is the ethical training of those who join the military. Its importance cannot be overestimated. Individuals must live with the ethical choices they make. In the military, these choices may entail the killing, maiming, or psychological scarring of an enemy or enemies. And whether a human being is an enemy or an ally, he or she remains a unique human person. Because it is important for

Introduction

soldiers to have a clear conscience and a sense of personal integrity, soldiers need to be able to justify actions that they take. They need to be able to conclude that their actions are morally correct; if not they will suffer a lifetime of guilt and recrimination. Members of the armed forces also need to understand the moral significance of ethical conduct. Through ethical conduct individuals become morally good; unethical actions undermine a person's moral goodness.

It would be an error to think that military ethics are important only to members of the armed forces. Since members of the military carry out their responsibilities on behalf of the citizens of the nation they represent, the ethical standards embraced by the armed forces reflect on the entire populace in whose name those forces conduct themselves. In order to act ethically, members of the military need to understand *why* they need to do the right thing as well as *how* to determine in what the right decision consists. Ordinarily, given the structure of the military chain of command, the right decision consists in obeying one's senior officer. Occasionally, however, the right thing to do is to refuse orders and to report one's commanding officer to a superior officer because an improper order was issued. And while it is true that soldiers are punished for disobeying orders, it is also true that soldiers risk being punished if they follow illegal orders. Therefore, it is immensely important for soldiers to understand what constitutes a legal order and why an illegal order merits the illegal designation. Being able to make these types of distinctions requires, first, education about the nature of ethics and, second, reflection on cases of proper and improper military conduct, subjects central to this book.

The United States launched Operation Iraqi Freedom on March 19, 2003. Since that date hundreds of thousands of U.S. servicemen and women have performed with military distinction while observing the highest ethical standards. Regrettably, there have also been reported instances of questionable ethical behavior. In regard to the mistreatment of prisoners at Abu Ghraib prison, former U.S. senator Ben Nighthorse Campbell asked, "My first thought was, how in the hell did those people get in our Army?" Campbell, who served as a military policeman with the Air Force during the Korean War, remarked, concerning widely disseminated photos of detainees at Abu Ghraib being humiliated, that "An outside observer would spot those pictures and say, 'Those are Americans? What a bunch of degenerates.'" Campbell contended that the U.S. soldiers who abused Iraqi prisoners cast shame on any American in uniform. "I know the training I went through as a military air policeman. There was no way you could have done this…without knowing you were doing something wrong."[3]

In June and July 2006 accounts about an atrocity that was much worse than abuses committed at Abu Ghraib came to light. This case entailed the alleged killing of an Iraqi family following the rape of a fourteen-year-old girl, Abeer al-Janabi, by a group of four or five military personnel. On July 3, 2006, Steven Green, a twenty-one-year-old former Army private, was charged with murder in federal court in Charlotte, North Carolina.[4] Reporting about what allegedly happened follows:

> July 1, 2006, Baghdad—The U.S. Army is investigating allegations that American soldiers raped and killed a woman and killed three of her family members in a town south of Baghdad and then reported the incident as an insurgent attack, a military official said Friday.
>
> The alleged crimes occurred in March in the insurgent hotbed of Mahmoudiya. The four soldiers involved, from the 502nd Infantry Regiment, attempted to burn the family's home to the ground and blamed insurgents for the carnage, according to a military official familiar with the investigation.…
>
> No charges have been filed in the case, which the official said was "in the very early stages."
>
> Maj. Gen. James Thurman…ordered the investigation into the killings…according to a terse statement released by the military Friday. A preliminary inquiry "found sufficient information existed to recommend a criminal investigation into the incident," the statement said.[5]

While many instances of alleged misconduct have not yet been adjudicated, some cases have been resolved, with severe sentences handed down to those found guilty of wrongful conduct. A case in point occurred on January 21, 2006, when a high-ranking member of the U.S. armed forces was convicted of negligent homicide in the death of an Iraqi general:

> The highest-ranking U.S. Army officer charged with killing a detainee in Iraq was found guilty on Saturday of negligent homicide but not guilty on the more serious charge of murder of an Iraqi general during an interrogation.
>
> A jury of six Army officers convicted Chief Warrant Officer Lewis Welshofer Jr. in charges resulting from the suffocation death of Iraqi Maj. Gen. Abed Hamed Mowhoush.
>
> The general was placed head-first in a sleeping bag as Welshofer covered his mouth and sat on his chest during a fatal interrogation in November 2003. Prosecutors accused Welshofer of using harsh techniques to try to get information from Mowhoush, describing them as "torture."[6]

The abuse of prisoners in the custody of the U.S. military and the wrongful deaths of Iraqis at the hands of U.S. personnel represent egregious ethical misconduct. In some cases, the men and women who acted wrongly knew what they were doing was immoral and did it anyway. Ethical education would not have made a difference in these cases.

In many other situations, however, ignorance, confusion, or mistaken trust in a superior's order led to unethical conduct. Circumstances such as these point to the need for comprehensive and practical ethics education for military personnel.

One of the obligations of the political leadership that commits the United States to war, and of the military strategists who plan tactics to bring about victory over an enemy, is to make certain that those who wage war do so without undermining their personal integrity. It goes without saying that the nation's honor is inextricably tied to the conduct of its armed forces and that neither soldier nor nation pursues justice alone.

CHAPTER ONE
THE JUST WAR TRADITION

We live in an imperfect world, in which there is an abundance of injustice, prejudice, violence, and disrespect. These negatives can characterize the relationships among individuals as well as those among nation-states, ethnic and religious groups, and various types of hostile factions such as the majority Shiite Muslims and the minority Sunni Muslims in Iraq. The ways to overcome hatred and conflict are through promotion of understanding, rejection of violence, and willingness to get beyond past differences. The path to peace, however, is often rejected as conflicting parties choose confrontation over negotiation and compromise.

When nations choose not to resolve their differences through compromise and resort instead to war, many seemingly compelling reasons can be given for that decision. A case is usually made by the nation that declares war that war is a last resort, the only remaining option. Citizens tend to agree with decisions to go to war if these decisions rest on valid grounds. Such valid grounds as the necessity of repelling unjust aggressors or defending an ally are generally accepted as defensible reasons for going to war.

In 2003, with Operation Iraqi Freedom, U.S. President George W. Bush cited a different rationale in support of military action against Iraq. President Bush said that he was convinced that the Iraqi political leadership was developing weapons of mass destruction, which would likely be used against the United States. In order to prevent possible future attacks by Iraq or by terrorists who were supplied by Iraq with weapons of mass destruction, Bush decided to *preemptively* attack that nation, drive Iraqi President Saddam Hussein from power, and destroy Iraqi capacity to launch nuclear, chemical, or biological weapons. With preemption, a nation is not fighting back and repelling an

1

aggressor force. Rather, a nation is anticipating that it will be attacked and is acting to prevent the attack. The anticipation of an attack is based on classified intelligence. Therefore, a preemptive attack is justifiable if the intelligence that prompts it is accurate. In an ultimatum to Iraq on March 17, 2003, President Bush said, "Intelligence gathered by this and other governments leaves no doubt that the Iraq regime continues to possess and conceal some of the most lethal weapons ever devised."[1] President Bush reiterated his belief that he was acting on sound information when he addressed the citizens of the United States on March 19, 2003.

> Our nation enters this conflict reluctantly—yet, our purpose is sure. The people of the United States and our friends and allies will not live at the mercy of an outlaw regime that threatens the peace with weapons of mass murder. We will meet that threat now, with our Army, Air Force, Navy, Coast Guard and Marines, so that we do not have to meet it later with armies of fire fighters and police and doctors on the streets of our cities.
>
> Now that conflict has come the only way to limit its duration is to apply decisive force. And I assure you, this will not be a campaign of half measures, and we will accept no outcome but victory.[2]

One could say that the history of humankind is a history of war. Some of the reasons that wars were fought in the past, however, would be rejected today. For example, the Crusades, which took place between the eleventh and thirteenth centuries, were carried out in order to reclaim the Christian shrines of the Holy Land from the Muslims who occupied this territory and controlled access to the Christian shrines. Beginning in the 1500s, the nations of Western Europe, such as England, France, and Spain, used warfare against nations whose territory they wanted to annex or acquire. In the Middle Ages, knights went to war against knights who were pledged to other lords to avenge perceived wrongs or to settle scores. Wars fought for religious reasons, wars of aggression to subjugate nondeveloped nations or to satisfy the ego of a leader would not be considered justifiable in the contemporary world.

Up until recently, wars have generally involved opposing military forces. These forces wore uniforms and were in the service of one side or the other. Members of the military belonged to clearly differentiated branches of the military services, such as the Army, Navy, Marines, or Air Force, and within those branches they could be further delineated by their training for special kinds of missions. Thus, the U.S. Army has Green Beret troops who carry out very dangerous and complex missions, and the Navy has Seals whose work is highly skilled and includes unconventional warfare and counterterrorism attacks.

During the past fifty years warfare has undergone radical changes. During the Vietnam War, the Viet Cong used guerrilla tactics. These tactics included dispensing with uniforms and using nontraditional-age fighters to prosecute the war. Hence, sometimes children threw hand grenades at U.S. military personnel, or Vietnamese old men, women, and people in wheel chairs were armed and prepared to engage in surprise unconventional attacks.

The terrorist strike of 9/11 in the United States prompted warlike tactics in retaliation. However, the look of warfare today is very different from what it was during the Allied invasion of Normandy in 1945, a classic military undertaking.

The Normandy invasion was directed by U.S. Gen. Dwight D. Eisenhower. On June 6, 1944, at five beaches on the Normandy coast of France, 156,000 U.S., British, and Canadian troops landed and proceeded inland. Before the invasion, Allied planes pounded the Nazi defenders and dropped thousands of paratroopers behind German lines the night before the seaborne landings. Local French Resistance forces, alerted to the imminent invasion, engaged in behind-the-lines sabotage against the occupying Germans. German failure to successfully defend the Normandy area from the Allied liberation forces doomed Hitler's dream of a Nazi-controlled Europe and marked the beginning of the end for Germany. Normandy represented a spectacular military victory in that the Allies persisted and the Nazis could not keep up against a superior opponent. Tragically, the number killed, wounded, or missing in the entire campaign was estimated as in excess of 400,000.[3]

In the history of warfare there have been many kinds of changes, but during the twentieth century these changes proceeded at a rapid rate. World War I was fought in Europe from 1914 to 1918. At its outset, soldiers were mounted on horseback and carried rifles; by its conclusion, weapons were fired from armored tanks and aircraft. Weapons of war changed dramatically with the advent of the atomic bomb in 1945 and laser-guided missiles in the 1980s.

Up until the Vietnam War of the 1960s and early 1970s, there were some constants in war. Members of the military wore uniforms and engaged each other. Military skill was about fighting enemy forces, and the armed forces that survived in greater number, having removed an opponent's ability to continue to do battle, were considered victorious.

In World War II, in the 1940s, many cities were bombed, leading to thousands of civilian casualties. Both the Allied and Axis powers engaged in saturation bombing, with cities such as London, England; Dresden, Germany; and Tokyo, Japan, suffering major loss of life and destruction of property. The most significant and most remembered bombings of World War II, however, were the atomic bomb attacks authorized by U.S. President Harry Truman and carried out against Hiroshima, Japan, on August 5, 1945, and, three days later, against Nagasaki, Japan. The combined death toll from these atomic bombings is estimated at more than 300,000 people.

In the past few decades, armed conflict changed with the emergence of terrorism on a worldwide scale. Terrorists challenge political and military leaders to figure out who the terrorists are, where they meet, what kinds of weapons they have, and what kinds of attacks they could launch. They operate in cells, sometimes connected to and financed by a leadership group and sometimes independently, and, for the most part, they are successful at avoiding detection.

Whether or not terrorists should be considered the equivalent of military personnel is an open question. Terrorists look like everyone else; they generally try to blend into communities so that they do not raise suspicions and so that they can carry out attacks without being thwarted. In the aftermath of the attacks of 9/11, President George W. Bush declared a war on terrorism and, in order to defeat terrorism, decided to deploy the U.S. military in Afghanistan on October 7, 2001, and in Iraq on March 19, 2003. There is debate about the merits of saying whether or not terrorists should be considered the equivalent of an enemy force in a conventional war and whether or not calling an attack against terrorists a war is appropriate. This is an issue that will not soon be resolved. For now, let us proceed as though terrorists are enemy combat forces and grant that the United States, and many other nations, are at war with terrorists and terrorism.

On June 29, 2006, in considering the case of *Hamdan v. Rumsfeld,* the U.S. Supreme Court by a five-to-three majority (with one abstention) advanced the thinking that captured alleged terrorists should be accorded similar procedural safeguards as those given to prisoners taken in the course of traditional wars. Salim Ahmed Hamdan, a prisoner at a U.S.-operated detention facility at Guantánamo Bay, Cuba, sought the Supreme Court's agreement that prisoners are entitled to judicial proceedings that afford them legal protections that the Bush administration did not want to grant them. Judicial guarantees required by the decision are cited in the following newspaper account:

> While Common Article 3 provides fewer safeguards than other portions of the Geneva Convention, it does prohibit the "passing of sentences" without a judgment from "a regularly constituted court affording all the judicial guarantees which are recognized as indispensable by civilized peoples."
>
> The article also holds that a humanitarian agency, such as the Red Cross, may be called to ensure that the Geneva protections are being obeyed, although the provision is not mandatory.[4]

Ultimately, what needs to be done is to advance an understanding of why fighting should be done within the context of the just war tradition and why it is important to limit harm regardless of who the enemy is.

For as long as people have disagreed with one another, there have been physical altercations. In chapter 4 of the Book of Genesis, we read an account of homicide:

> Cain said to his brother Abel, "Let us go out to the field." And when they were in the field, Cain rose up against his brother Abel, and killed him.
> Then the Lord said to Cain, "Where is your brother Abel?" He said, "I do not know; am I my brother's keeper?"
> And the Lord said, "What have you done? Listen; your brother's blood is crying out to me from the ground!"(Gen 4:8–10)

For as long as groups of people have had problems with one another, there have been battles between them to resolve their problems.

For more than two thousand years, alongside the hostility and fighting of war, there has been a parallel development aimed at limiting the violence of war and ensuring, as far as possible, the well-being of those who are not involved in the war. This development is called "the just war tradition" and the rules that emerged from the tradition are known as "the just war criteria."

At the outset, when people outside the military confronted military and political leaders with the goal of restraining war, a compilation of the rules of war was not the objective. Rather, a pragmatic immediate goal was in view: to restrain warfare so as to protect those not involved in the fighting and to ensure the well-being of the community. As it happened, however, since the seventeenth century, the various initiatives undertaken to lessen the harms of war coalesced into an internationally accepted list of rules that govern both the decision to go to war and the ways in which wars are prosecuted.

The need to limit the violence of war is self-evident. As long ago as the fourth century, Augustine wrote, "The passion for inflicting harm, the cruel thirst for vengeance, an unpacific and relentless spirit, the fever of revolt, the lust of power, and suchlike things, all these are rightly condemned in war."[5] Whether or not restraint can be practiced as wars unfold is debatable, and whether or not the rules of war should be applied to military responses to terrorism is a question of our times. Perhaps it will be easier to address these questions after we have considered how the just war criteria came into being and the shape the current formulations of these criteria takes.

Major Benchmarks in the Development of the Just War Tradition

Declaration of War. The first development in the just war tradition is attributed to Cicero, a Roman philosopher and orator, who lived in the century before the birth of Jesus, more than two thousand years ago. Cicero demanded the articulation of a formal declaration of war by the king or emperor. The reasons for a declaration of war are twofold: first, to possibly prevent a war by giving an opponent a clear statement of grievances against him or his nation so as to convince the offending party of the need to desist from belligerent activities; and second, to lay out for one's own followers a convincing argument as to why offensive military tactics are called for.[6]

Constantine. For the first three hundred years of Christianity, Christians considered themselves pacifists. They thought that the teachings of Jesus in the New Testament forbade them to take up arms and kill, and so they practiced pacifism. In AD 313, Constantine, the Roman emperor, issued the Edict of Milan, which granted official recognition to Christianity. Christians then began to see things differently and became willing to take up arms to defend the state, of which they were now privileged citizens. In view of the fact that Christianity became one of the major religions of the world, and that Christian denominations are major religions in the developed Western world, the fact that Christians are willing warriors is one of the principal reasons that

7

there have been so many wars throughout history. (It is true that some Christians, such as the Quakers, the Amish, and the Mennonites, are pacifists and will not fight in wars, but these particular Christian religions do not have large numbers of followers.)

Saint Augustine (354–430). In 387, Augustine became a Christian, and in 390 he became a bishop in Hippo, a city in North Africa. A brilliant philosopher and theologian, Augustine exercised significant influence on Christian theology.

Since one of the central teachings of Christianity is love of neighbor, and since Augustine connects the military service with the love of one's fellow citizens and the love of noncombatants in the enemy camp, a major theoretical issue of why a Christian can be a warrior is resolved. Christian warriors are required by the mandate that they love their neighbors to take up arms to defend these neighbors from harm, while sparing noncombatants who are citizens of the enemy nation the danger of being attacked. Augustine explained to fighters that "the commandment forbidding killing was not broken by those who waged wars on the authority of God...."[7] However, the only persons who can legitimately be killed in a just war are enemy combatants because they are agents of a sovereign who has breached peace and good order between states.

Peace of God. In the tenth century the Peace of God was formulated specifically for the purpose of instructing knight-warriors that certain classes of people should not suffer attack during the wars that the knights were fighting. The protected classes included women, children, clergy, pilgrims, merchants, physicians, nurses, teachers, the aged, and the infirm—in short, noncombatants. The reasoning for the Peace of God was that civilians are a separate class and should be spared the fate of combatants.[8] Also included in the Peace of God are consecrated places, such as churches, monasteries, and cemeteries, in which hostilities are not to take place. Fighting during consecrated times, such as Sundays and feast days, was forbidden. Church authorities penalized those who violated the terms of the Peace of God with excommunication, that is, removal from the ranks of Christian believers. At that time, during the Middle Ages, the penalty of excommunication was much feared, as most Christians truly valued their membership in the church.

Truce of God. The Truce of God dates from the eleventh century. It arose amid the anarchy of feudalism as a remedy for the powerlessness of lay authorities to enforce respect for the public peace. At that time there was an epidemic of private wars, which made Europe a battlefield bristling with fortified castles and overrun by armed bands who respected nothing, not even sanctuaries, clergy, or consecrated days. The Council of Elne in 1027 issued a canon, or rule, concerning the sanctification of Sunday and forbade hostilities from Saturday night until Monday morning. (Elne was a city in France; church councils are frequently identified by the location in which the meeting was held.) This canon was the precursor of the Truce of God. The prohibition was subsequently extended to the days of great religious solemnity such as Christmas and Easter and many other days of religious observance. Efforts were made in this way to limit the scourge of private war without suppressing it outright. The truce soon spread from France to Italy and Germany and, by the twelfth century, to the whole Christian Church. The problem of establishing a public peace, which was a great desire of the Middle Ages, was not resolved at one stroke, but an impetus was given with the Truce of God. Gradually, public authorities, royalty, and leagues of nobles became less warlike and began to think that war should be restricted to international conflicts.[9]

Chivalry. In the Middle Ages men from a privileged class called "knights" fought wars; knights were required to observe a code known as "chivalry." In its simplest terms, chivalry demanded that fighters respect women and those who were weak and that they restrict warlike actions to opponents such as infidels (Moslems who had taken over religious sites) or knights who were loyal to different lords. From chivalry is derived the idea of the fair fight, as well as the notion that a warrior's integrity is tied to his observance of strict rules regarding civilians.

Use of the Crossbow. When the crossbow was developed in the Middle Ages, Pope Urban II (1035–1099) forbade its use against Christians. So did the Second Lateran Council, which stated, "We prohibit under anathema that murderous art of crossbowmen and archers, which is hateful to God, to be employed against Christians and Catholics from now on" (1139).[10] One reason the use of the crossbow was forbidden in war was that the weapon was deployed from a distance to kill someone who could not be seen; it was considered murder to annihilate an opponent with an arrow rather than give the opponent the chance to fight back in a combat situation, because combat was a feature of knightly fighting. James Turner Johnson offers a second reason bows and arrows were banned, a reason that harkens back to the code of chivalry:

> The weapons named in the ban were precisely those most likely to be employed by soldiers who were not of the nobility, and in particular by mercenaries. This suggests that the ban on these weapons was intended to limit the circle of persons to be engaged in war, that is, to restrict war to members of the knightly class.[11]

Thomas Aquinas (circa 1225–1274). A Dominican friar who is recognized by the Catholic Church as a saint, Thomas Aquinas contributed significantly to the development of just war theory. In his *Summa Theologica,* Thomas specified three criteria that need to be met for a just war: right authority (a sovereign government rather than individuals declaring and conducting the war), just cause (to avenge wrongs or to restore what was unjustly seized), and right intention (the advancement of good or the avoidance of evil), while also laying the groundwork for other criteria that would eventually be integrated into the tradition.[12] One of Aquinas's major contributions to the development of moral analysis was his formulation of the principle of the double effect. According to this principle, moral acts are defended as righteous because of the intention of the moral agent. If a soldier intends to save his own life, or defend himself, and in order to do so kills an enemy soldier who is about to attack him, the action of the soldier who acts in self-defense is morally appropriate. Killing the enemy is tolerated and not directly intended. If the soldier could have defended himself without such a dire outcome, he would have done so. Thomas Aquinas thus argued that the justification for self-defense rests with the intention of an individual who is motivated by a reasonable goal rather than the unworthy intention of harming or killing another.

Franciscus De Victoria (1480–1546). Victoria (whose name is also given as Vitoria) was a Catholic theologian and scholar who wrote two influential books in the sixteenth century. In *De Indis* and *De Jure Belli,* Victoria was at the forefront of a movement that was instrumental in producing international law as a secular science.[13] His contention that political power comes from the people who make up the state, rather than from God, became a foundational principle of modern politics. Victoria believed that God's law provides moral legitimacy for the *jus gentium,* that is, human law, but his writings opened up the possibility of human law standing on its own, without justification of its precepts based on the will of God. Following Victoria, evaluations of wars as just or unjust became less a task of the church and more an occupation of agents in secular society such as monarchs, politicians, philosophers, journalists, and citizens.

Many wars before Victoria's time were fought for religious reasons, such as the Crusades and attacks against native peoples to subjugate them before converting them. Victoria argued that religiously based wars cannot be justified and that the extension of an empire or the personal glory of the king were equally unworthy reasons to wage war. He said that the defense of one's nation and its people are the only reasons to go to war. Additionally, Victoria argued for an idea that is called "comparative justice." According to James Turner Johnson, "When neither side can be unqualifiedly certain of the justice of its cause, it is that much more bound to observe scrupulously the limits set in the *jus in bello.*"[14] (The Latin phrase *jus in bello* means justice, or appropriateness, in fighting.)

As for the decision to go to war, Victoria believed that a prince should seek wise counsel in coming to such a momentous undertaking. If citizens consider the war manifestly unjust, "they should refuse to serve, even though this means refusal to obey their sovereign."[15]

Grotius. Hugo Grotius (1583–1645) was a Dutch jurist and humanist who wrote at the time of the Thirty Years War (1618–1648). His book *De jure belli ac pacis* (1625) continued in the vein of Victoria and represented a "metamorphosis of just war thought."[16] Building his analysis of the morality of war on a secular concept of natural law, Grotius theorized, "The way to discover what is required by nature is to observe how nations of men think and act."[17] Grotius counseled that there should be moderation in war. His ideas led to the conclusion that, since war is a secular activity, theological differences separating Catholics from Protestants should not be considered as a justification for war.[18] Thus, the modern state had the right to wage war, and wars were to be fought with humanitarian sensitivity as well as a due regard for civilization. We trace to Grotius a movement from regulation of war based on religious ideals and notions of chivalry to an international legal basis in natural law that recognized the military as a specialized segment of society with responsibility for prosecuting wars. Interestingly, Grotius understood that wars could as easily be unjust as just. "If the cause of war should be unjust," he wrote, "even if the war should have been undertaken in a lawful way, all acts which arise therefrom are unjust."[19]

Clausewitz. Carl von Clausewitz (1780–1831) was a Prussian military strategist who is best known for a book he wrote that was published posthumously. In *On War* Clausewitz made the case that war is prosecuted by the state, which seeks to bring sufficient force to bear to achieve its purpose, that is, victory. This straightforward approach to military tactics does not create a place for von Clausewitz in the survey of those people and agreements that constitute markers in the development of restraint of war. In fact, von Clausewitz wrote that "to introduce into the philosophy of war itself a principle of moderation would be an absurdity."[20] Instead, one idea that von Clausewitz fleshed out in regard to the deliberations of political leaders who are deciding to go to war had an impact on the development of the just war tradition.

Von Clausewitz, in treating ends and means in strategy and war, implied that a certain proportionality should exist between the scale of effort, cost, and risk a state would reasonably accept and the value of objectives it intended to achieve as a result of the war. If the war would enact too much destruction for the side that was starting it, the war should not be started, and the nation's leaders needed to understand that making this calculation was their duty.

Von Clausewitz thought that states would show less inclination to approach the extremes of violence and to exert themselves to the point of exhaustion in a war if they made clear-headed calculations in advance and considered whether a goal was worth pursuing. Proportionality needed to be taken into account by leaders who decided to prosecute wars, and the realization that the desired goal could be disproportionate to the projected human costs could deter leaders from engaging in wars.[21]

Lieber Code. Francis Lieber (1798–1872) was born in Germany and emigrated to the United States. In 1863, while a professor at Columbia University, Dr. Lieber, a jurist and political philosopher, wrote a document called the *Code for the Government of Armies in the Field,* and President Abraham Lincoln and the Union War Department adhered to the principles Lieber formulated. Popularly referred to as the "Lieber Code,"[22] Dr. Lieber's work continues the transition from medieval rationale about restraining violence to a modern, secular rationale.

A significant criterion in the Lieber Code is General Orders No. 100, which accords to militias and volunteer corps rights similar to armies, provided that these forces have a commander who is responsible for his subordinates, that they wear distinctive garb recognizable from a distance, that they carry arms openly, and that they conduct their operations in accordance with the laws of war.[23] Thus, the Confederate Army, which opposed the Union Army in the U.S. Civil War, was viewed as a legitimate fighting force that could reasonably engage in combat. With regard to restraint of violence, "Lieber explicitly denied the right to inflict additional wounds or to kill enemy soldiers already wounded."[24]

One area in which the just war tradition may have been weakened during the 1860s is in regard to noncombatants. The weapons used in the Civil War and such campaigns as Sherman's march across Georgia to the sea put noncombatants in harm's way. Additionally, the soldiers who did the fighting were not from a privileged military class, as had been the case in the Middle Ages, and many of them were paid mercenaries who fought to make money rather than to uphold ideals.

Geneva Convention (1863). In 1863 delegates from sixteen nations met in Geneva, Switzerland, to attempt to reach a consensus regarding the wartime treatment of wounded military personnel as well as those who cared for or sheltered them. Since the United States was in the midst of the Civil War, no U.S. delegates attended the conference.

The knowledge that some persons who wear military uniforms do not wage war or present a threat led to an agreement for the "Amelioration of the Condition of the Wounded and Sick," which was adopted by twelve nations and which subsequently became a standard with widespread acceptance. This agreement, which also recognized the work of the International Red Cross, established that military personnel who are members of medical corps would be considered neutral and not subject to warring actions. Furthermore, wounded soldiers or sailors would be given humane treatment and not attacked, and civilians who assist or shelter the wounded would be regarded as neutral and not be attacked. Wearing the international emblem of the Red Cross would identify those who were taking care of wounded, and this insignia would entitle them to protection.

Hague Convention (1907). The purpose of the Hague Convention was mainly to restrain ever more deadly weapons of war and set out requirements for irregular troops, that is, those not part of a national army. Summarizing the Hague requirements, James Turner Johnson writes:

> The laws, rights, and duties of war apply not only to armies, but also to militia and volunteer corps fulfilling the following conditions:

1. To be commanded by a person responsible for his subordinates;
2. to have a fixed distinctive emblem recognizable at a distance;
3. to carry arms openly, and
4. to conduct their operations in accordance with the laws and customs of war.[25]

In regard to weapons, the Hague Convention forbade the use of poison gas against opposing forces.

Geneva Convention (1929). In ninety-seven articles, many aspects of the treatment of prisoners of war were clarified. Detailed rules about such matters as hygiene, food, clothing, religious practices, recreation, and the handling of prisoners' mail and parcels were laid out. The subject of prison camp discipline and penalties for violations of camp rules were taken up, as was the matter of repatriation of prisoners of war. The International Committee of the Red Cross was entrusted with the task of sending delegates to prisoner of war camps to observe conditions and to transmit information on prisoners. Acknowledging the need to arrange peaceable surroundings for those no longer engaged in combat, namely prisoners, was the primary contribution of this meeting. By achieving reciprocity among nations, warring parties benefited from this type of agreement.

Nuremberg Principles (1948). During World War II there were horrific crimes committed against civilians by individual Nazis whose defense for their misconduct was that they were following orders. After World War II, an international tribunal in Nuremberg, Germany, tried those accused of the most egregious crimes. One of the actions taken by the tribunal was to state unequivocally that there is a fundamental moral law that binds all rational persons and that those rational persons should refuse orders to harm civilians or prisoners of war. Even if the internal law of Nazi Germany required German civilian or military personnel to perform inhumane actions, those who served in the administration of German prison camps or in the Nazi military still bore responsibility for their conduct under international law, as did the German head of state. To make themselves perfectly clear, the members of the tribunal defined crimes against peace, war crimes, and crimes against humanity, as quoted following:

a. Crimes against peace:
    i. Planning, preparation, initiation or waging of a war of aggression or a war in violation of international treaties, agreements or assurances;
    ii. Participation in a common plan or conspiracy for the accomplishment of any of the acts mentioned under (i).
b. War crimes:
    Violations of the laws or customs of war which include, but are not limited to, murder, ill-treatment or deportation to slave-labor or for any other purpose of civilian population of or in occupied territory, murder or ill treatment of prisoners of war, of persons on the seas, killing of hostages, plunder of public or private property, wanton destruction of cities, towns, or villages, or devastation not justified by military necessity.
c. Crimes against humanity:
    Murder, extermination, enslavement, deportation and other inhuman acts done against any civilian population, or persecutions on political, racial or religious grounds, when such acts are done or such persecutions are carried on in execution of or in connection with any crime against peace or any war crime.[26]

Universal Declaration of Human Rights. On December 10, 1948, the General Assembly of the United Nations adopted a document known as the *Universal Declaration of Human Rights.* This statement represented a breakthrough, which came when leaders throughout the world proclaimed the rights that humans have because they are human and the responsibilities of governments to affirm and protect these rights. The *Universal Declaration* stands as an historic benchmark that specifies rights of women, minorities, and all peoples to work, vote, participate in government, receive an education, and a range of other rights. Of particular interest to us within the purview of restraint of hostilities in time of war are articles 5 and 10:

> Article 5. No one shall be subjected to torture or to cruel, inhuman or degrading treatment or punishment.

> Article 10. Everyone is entitled in full equality to a fair and public hearing by an independent and impartial tribunal, in the determination of his rights and obligations and of any criminal charge against him.[27]

Geneva Convention (1949). At the Geneva meeting in 1949, four conventions, each with numerous articles, were adopted. Each convention protects a different group at risk during armed conflict and specifies how that group must be humanely treated. The four groups specified by those agreeing to the conventions of 1949 are

> The First Convention—wounded and sick members of the armed forces in the field;
> The Second Convention—wounded, sick, and shipwrecked members of the armed forces at sea as well as shipwreck victims;
> The Third Convention—prisoners of the war;
> The Fourth Convention—civilians in times of war.[28]

Common Article 3 of the Geneva Conventions of 1949 holds that

> in the case of armed conflict not of an international character occurring in the territory of one of the High Contracting Parties, each Party to the conflict shall be bound to apply, as a minimum, the following provisions:

> (A) Persons taking no active part in the hostilities, including members of armed forces who have laid

down their arms and those placed *'hors de combat'* by sickness, wounds, detention, or any other cause, shall in all circumstances be treated humanely, without any adverse distinction founded on race, colour, religion or faith, sex, birth or wealth, or any other similar criteria.

To this end, the following acts are and shall remain prohibited at any time and in any place whatsoever with respect to the above-mentioned persons:

(a) violence to life and person, in particular murder of all kinds, mutilation, cruel treatment and torture;
(b) taking of hostages;
(c) outrages upon personal dignity, in particular humiliating and degrading treatment;
(d) the passing of sentences and the carrying out of executions without previous judgment pronounced by a regularly constituted court, affording all the judicial guarantees which are recognized as indispensable by civilized peoples.[29]

Protocols to Geneva Conventions (1977). Given the ability of political and military leaders to use weapons of mass destruction that posed unimaginable threats to civilian populations, a consensus was reached at Geneva in 1977 to warn against use of such weapons.[30] A lengthy and detailed document, the protocols also gave directions for medical treatment of persons in occupied territories in accordance with widely held standards of medical ethics, care for children who become separated from their families, special status for airplanes that serve medical purposes, and humane treatment of prisoners, even if these people have not belonged to the armed forces of a recognized opponent. Jean de Preux writes about how the 1977 document broke new ground:

The Protocol...goes beyond the established rules in that it prohibits attacks against the civilian population and civilian objects by way of reprisals, provides

unequivocally for the protection of objects which constitute the cultural or spiritual heritage of peoples,
states that starvation of civilians as a method of warfare
is prohibited, (and) forbids the use of methods or
means of warfare which are intended or may be
expected to cause widespread, long-term and severe
damage to the natural environment and thereby to
prejudice the health or survival of the population....
Those in charge of military operations must take the
necessary precautions to ensure respect for these provisions and ascertain that attacks are directed against
the adversary and not against civilians.[31]

*International Criminal Tribunals for the Former Yugoslavia and
Rwanda* (1993 and 1994). In 1993 and 1994, following accounts
of the rape of women by military personnel in Yugoslavia and
Rwanda, the tribunals set up to try war criminals specifically codified for the first time as a recognizable and independent crime
the rape of women in conquered territories.[32] No longer can military personnel erroneously think that part of the spoils of war is
to assault and degrade the women who are on the losing side.

Jus ad Bellum: Right to Wage War, or Law on the Use of Force

War is a dreadful enterprise. Military personnel and civilians
die and are maimed. Property is destroyed, natural environments
are fouled, and civilians and military personnel suffer from dislocation and mental illnesses. There are enormous economic
costs as well, with money that could have been used to build up
communities and meet human needs instead of used to kill
people and destroy places.

Because of the predictable horrors of war, a question naturally arises: If wars cause so much suffering, why do we have wars,
and how can our leaders justify decisions to commit nations to
war? The *jus ad bellum* is a Latin phrase that encompasses several

criteria that political leaders need to meet before they can claim to act in good faith when committing a nation to war. These criteria are rules that have evolved from the benchmarks we surveyed and that have a common goal of keeping wars from happening in the first place, and, if that is not possible, limiting the harms of war.

There are many different formulations of the *jus ad bellum* criteria; I build on those developed by the Pew Foundation because they contain the essence of what the *jus ad bellum* has come to mean.

First, the decision to go to war must be declared by a lawful authority.[33]

Private individuals and groups are not permitted to take up arms against others, however justified their cause may appear. Only governments, and this *may* include revolutionary leaders, may wage war, and they must do it openly and legally.[34] The reason for the requirement that legitimate authority decide on warfare is obvious: in democracies, elected officials speak for the electorate, and in nondemocracies the power wielded by a king or other leader is acknowledged by the king's subjects and the broader international community. Cicero's insistence on a declaration of war as well as the thinking of Francis Lieber and the Hague Convention of 1907 about leaders of revolutionary movements are incorporated in this criterion.

Second, the cause must be just.

A government may wage war in self-defense, in defense of another nation, or to protect innocents. In past times, to regain something wrongfully taken was considered a valid reason to wage war, but this justification is not held contemporaneously. The desire for personal glory or revenge, or to impose tyrannical rule, or to impose a religion or punish a religion, or a nonreligious society, is not an acceptable cause for waging war.[35] In view of the fact that war causes so much harm and suffering, there should be a presumption against going to war and a reluctance to commit troops to military operations. Only the most severe and imminent threats against a nation should be considered a just cause for going to war.

Third, as the war progresses, a just intention should be evident in the strategy of war.[36]

The ultimate end of a government in waging war must be to establish peace rather than to suggest it is waging a just war when that government is actually pursuing its own gain.[37] Moreover, once the goal of the war has been achieved, such as the repelling of an aggressive force, the defending nation should cease hostilities so as to prevent additional harm and loss of life. Pursuant to the deliberations of tribunals that prosecuted war criminals from Nazi Germany and Yugoslavia and Rwanda, the concept of spoils of war, in which defeated nations are looted and their citizens raped or harmed in other ways, are identified as violating this criterion. Continued combat against enemy forces when it can reasonably be assumed that these forces lack the ability to fight on and are close to surrendering is likewise a violation.

Fourth, war must be a last resort and the only possible means of securing justice.

A governing authority must reasonably exhaust all diplomatic and nonmilitary options for securing peace before resorting to force. These attempts must represent real efforts and not be merely public relations exercises.[38] While international organizations such as the United Nations proceed slowly and are frequently inefficient due to bureaucratic constraints, last resort requires that the leaders of a nation who consider declaring war be patient and try every possible strategy to avoid going to war.

Fifth, there must be a reasonable chance of victory.

A government may not resort to war unless its prospects for success are good. In this way, lives will not be needlessly wasted in the pursuit of a hopeless cause.[39] Therefore, even if a nation has a just cause for going to war, if it would be overmatched and its defeat is predictable, the nation's leaders would not be justified in declaring war. Von Clausewitz, who wrote about military strategy, stating that an effective war plan demands sufficient force to achieve the goal of victory, implicitly endorsed this rationale. If a nation cannot anticipate victory, it should not start or join a war.

Sixth, the good probably to be achieved by victory must outweigh the probable evil effects of the war.

A government must respond to aggression with force only when the effects of its defensive actions will not leave it in a more compromised condition. This is a hard calculation to make, but the predictable death, injuries, destruction, dislocation, and mental distress associated with war must be evaluated before the decision to enter armed conflict is reached.[40] Additionally, wars for such reasons as to depose tyrants or destroy terrorist infrastructure should not be undertaken unless a calculation can be made that the situation at the end of hostilities will be significantly better than that before the hostilities.

Jus in Bello: Acceptable Behavior in War

Jus in bello are criteria that dictate what members of the military may do in the conduct of war. Soldiers are equipped with uniforms and weapons, but their uniforms symbolize a mission and they are not allowed to do whatever they want with their weapons. Just war tradition describes acceptable behavior by military personnel as they prosecute wars. These criteria are as follows.

First, only right means may be employed in the conduct of war, and only enemy combatants may be the targets of direct attack.[41]

Those who wage war are morally obligated to discriminate between combatants and noncombatants. While civilians unfortunately may sometimes come in harm's way, in accordance with the principle of double effect, military personnel may never intentionally target them.[42] Members of the military who fight wars may not attack civilians, even if they are ordered to do so by their commanders. Attacking civilians is a war crime and cannot be justified within the context of the just war criteria or such agreements as the United Nations *Universal Declaration on Human Rights.* In the Middle Ages the Peace of God and the norms of chivalry sought to protect civilians. As times and weapons of war changed, the status of civilians as noncombatants did not change. Consequently, military personnel should never directly target

22

civilians. Beyond this, military personnel should use right means in the conduct of war, meaning that chemical, biological, and nuclear weapons should not be used.

Second, as a war progresses, a just intention should be evident in the strategy of war.[43]

According to Augustine, "The wise man...will wage just wars (and) he will...lament the fact that he is faced with the necessity of waging just wars."[44] And Grotius contributed to the understanding of this criterion by declaring that soldiers should try to disable enemies, not kill them,[45] and should avoid what is shameful as well as what is strictly wrong "for that which is more just and better."[46] Thus, members of the armed forces, like the leaders who make the decision to go to war, should have for their goal to establish peace and, in so doing, to do as little harm as humanly possible.

Conclusion

Over the course of more than two thousand years, from Cicero's requirement that an emperor state the reasons for resorting to war, to the naming of rape as a war crime following civil wars in Yugoslavia and Rwanda, attempts have been made to limit the horrors of war. At different times in history, different parties have taken the lead in specifying what kinds of actions are unacceptable or what categories of people should not be attacked. As we have seen, these parties include emperors, kings, lords, church officials, theologians, philosophers, international jurists, military strategists, and humanitarian organizations.

The just war tradition that is the result of this assembled input is usually presented as just war criteria, similar to those stated earlier. In the United States the president and Congress are responsible for the calculations required by the *jus ad bellum,* that is, justifying the use of force against an adversary and estimating that a war, once started, will be successful. The U.S. Constitution authorizes Congress to declare war and the president, as commander-in-chief of the armed forces, is responsible to oversee the conduct of the war. The War Powers Act of 1973 spells out in detail how the executive and legislative branches of government should interact when the nation is at war.[47]

Historically, it is the president who has made the case to Congress for a declaration of war and, after due consideration, the Congress has acceded to the president's request. The president and Congress are burdened with an awesome responsibility as they commit the country to war, and frequently there are disagreements with decisions to start a war. In spite of the fact that national leaders try to rally support for war efforts and counsel a spirit of unanimity in times of war, the media airs positions of both agreement and disagreement with wars, and some members of Congress, who are at odds with the majority who favor the war, articulate the case against armed conflict.

Regardless of whether or not the country stands united behind a decision to go to war, the men and women of the armed forces fight wars. Leaders are largely responsible for the big picture, deciding that there is a just cause for a war, that it is a last resort that will likely result in more good than harm, and that the nation will be able to persist and win. Working through the elements of this big picture is enormously daunting and complicated, and it is carried out by a relatively small group of elected officials and their advisors.

Those who prosecute a war number in the hundreds of thousands (or more) and their responsibilities are much narrower than those of their elected leaders. Men and women who serve in the military are required to adhere to the *jus in bello* criteria, that is, to avoid harming civilians, to refuse to use forbidden weapons, and to exercise restraint by ceasing hostilities when victory is at hand. They should also refrain from harming prisoners of war and enemy troops who are wounded and present no threat.

The late senator Eugene McCarthy (D, MN), an outspoken critic of the war in Vietnam, regretted how little has been said about how the leaders' decisions impact the men and women in uniform. In 1975 McCarthy wrote:

> Too little has been said about the responsibility of the state to the soldier. This goes beyond the obligation for the soldier's welfare if he is wounded or when he

retires. It goes beyond the obligation for the care and support of his dependents. The state has a more fundamental obligation: to look to the justice and wisdom of the cause in which the soldier is committed.[48]

There is a chain of command in the military, and soldiers are trained to follow orders, which are issued by superiors. In the course of prosecuting wars, especially wars against terrorists, understanding which orders to follow and which to question presents a major challenge. In chapter 2 we reflect on how soldiers, sailors, members of the Air Force, the Coast Guard, Marines, and Reserves who carry out the actual fighting of a war should uphold their integrity while doing their duty.

Questions for Discussion

1. How does a preemptive war differ from a traditional war? Is it morally justifiable to fight a preemptive war?
2. How does a war against terrorists differ from a conventional war, and what kinds of ethical issues are raised by such a war?
3. Why have there been so many efforts throughout history to put limits on military forces in battle?
4. How does the role played by the International Red Cross in respect to prisoners of war serve humanitarian interests?
5. Why is it important to provide education about the just war tradition, and what groups should receive this education?
6. Select three individuals who contributed to the development of the just war tradition and describe the primary aspects of their contributions.
7. Choose three meetings that advanced the just war tradition and explain how actions taken at these meetings influenced the tradition.
8. What are the just war criteria? Which criteria apply to leaders of governments and which apply to troops on the ground? How do the *jus ad bellum* relate to the *jus in bello*?

9. Which requirements of the just war tradition could prevent wars from starting in the first place?

Case Study

A group of three U.S. soldiers has been separated from their company and has been fighting terrorists in an urban setting for six days. During this time their food and water supplies have been exhausted, and they have had little sleep because of the need to be vigilant. As the days have passed, more and more of the terrorists have been killed, and, for the past twenty-four hours, the three soldiers have not been fired upon. They decide to leave the shed-like building in which they have been hiding and attempt to make their way into the nearest town in an effort to be reunited with their company or other soldiers from their Army. Their spirits are not good because they are physically depleted, emotionally drained, and insecure without their platoon leader. As they make their way toward the nearby town, one of the three comes upon the body of an enemy terrorist and suggests to his companions that they decapitate and castrate the body, and hang the head on a fence in order to wear down the morale of any opposing fighters in the area who might come upon it. The other two U.S. soldiers do not know what to do or how they should react.

1. Based on the information presented in this chapter, what advice would you give the two soldiers who are unsure about what to do?
2 How would you evaluate the idea of the soldier who wants to castrate and decapitate the dead body and display it?
3. As gruesome and bizarre as this hypothetical case is, why might it be worth your time to consider such a case?

CHAPTER TWO

GOOD SOLDIERS: THEIR CONSCIENCES AND THEIR ACTIONS

Just wars do not just happen. Political and military leaders design them, and they are categorized as *just* if all the criteria enumerated in chapter 1 are met simultaneously. A burden on the president of the United States, who asks Congress for a declaration of war, is to reason to the conclusion that the war being considered would be just. Presidents ask for a great deal of information from advisors before requesting declarations of war, and many different types of counselors provide this information.

When the decision to go to war is taken, the majority of citizens tend to trust that the cause is just, recourse to arms is a last resort, there is a reasonable hope of a good outcome, and more good than evil will result from the undertaking. At the beginning of a war, it is difficult for a citizen or a soldier to substantiate an objection to the war decision because the commander-in-chief (the president) and that person's close advisors, as well as members of Congress, are the only ones who have access to the classified information that is crucial to the decision to go to war. Since in the United States the president and members of Congress are elected by the majority, there is a tendency to support these officials in such weighty matters. By so doing, democratic processes result in a stable system of government that allows for predictability and prosperity.

After a country goes to war, changes appear in society. There are many signs of patriotism, as people proclaim their allegiance to their country and support for its military. Those who question the decision to go to war, or the overall foreign policy that allows for war, usually find themselves in the minority and may be marginalized. Patriotism and militarism are much more apparent than dissent. Thus, in times of war, the majority of people concur

27

in the decision. Without support from the majority it would be impossible to staff the military or sustain the effort demanded by armed conflict.

Armed Conflict and Individual Members of the Armed Forces

In the United States the decision to go to war depends on the deliberations of elected officials, and support for the war comes from hundreds of millions of citizens. The actual prosecution of the war is the responsibility of the men and women who are members of the armed forces. These individuals face a two-pronged challenge: to perform their specific military responsibilities with competence, and to uphold ethical standards, so as to preserve their personal integrity along with the honor of the military.

What Is Morality?

Morality entails doing the right thing and being a good person. Those actions that promote human dignity and the well-being of society are morally right actions. Those actions that retard human dignity and the well-being of the group are morally wrong. Unfortunately, ethical conduct does not typically result in television coverage or newspaper headlines. What generally prompts people to think about the notion of morality in the military is the occasional aberrant behavior of an individual or group that shows blatant disregard for the rights of others and that tarnishes the reputation of the entire armed forces (that is, immoral behavior). Prisoner abuse at Abu Ghraib prison in Iraq constitutes a vivid example of egregiously immoral conduct.

At Abu Ghraib in November 2003, members of the 372nd Military Police Company from Pennsylvania were guarding Iraqi prisoners. Investigators have arrived at a general consensus that the prison was overcrowded, guards were not well trained to carry out their work, and oversight was lacking. Within this context some of the guards believed that their goal was to "soften up" the prisoners so that the prisoners would be conditioned to reveal important information about terrorist plots to members of interrogation teams. While the guards spoke of orders to soften up the detainees, it was difficult for investigators to document that higher-ups in the chain of command actually gave such orders. Also, clarifying what "to soften up" entailed was problematic because written instructions did not exist. The motivation for wanting to find out important information is obvious: learning what terrorist plots were in the planning stages would enable U.S. authorities to foil the plots and prevent deaths, injuries, and destruction of property. Understanding what methods of interrogation would be appropriate and what methods would be inappropriate, because these methods constituted torture or entailed inhumane degradation, was far less obvious. When pictures of U.S. servicemen and women abusing and humiliating naked Iraqi prisoners began to circulate in the United States and around the world in spring 2004, there was a protracted outcry. This triggered efforts to understand how such disturbingly immoral conduct could have occurred and to institute corrective measures to make certain that such conduct was not repeated in the future. A consensus began to emerge that members of the U.S. armed forces needed to be taught that the U.S. military repudiates the use of torture and of tactics that degrade enemy prisoners.

One of the participants in the Abu Ghraib prison scandal, Jeremy Sivits, was charged with one count of conspiracy to maltreat detainees, one count of dereliction, and two counts of maltreatment of detainees.[1] Sivits pleaded guilty to four criminal counts and agreed to testify against six other accused Americans. At his sentencing on May 19, 2004, at a special court martial in Baghdad, Sivits said, "I'd like to apologize to the Iraqi people and those detainees. I should have protected those detainees, not taken the photos." He was sentenced to one year of confinement and given a bad conduct discharge.

Sivits said that what he and the other military police did were all individual actions.[2] Sivits seems to have been implying that each individual bears responsibility for his or her actions, and he was admitting that what he did was wrong. If that were the case, he affirmed that some kinds of actions, such as torturing and humiliating prisoners, are ethically wrong and that he violated his professional code by going along with these actions. Nearly sixty years after the Nuremberg trials, which proclaimed that there exist objective standards that military personnel should affirm, Pvt. Jeremy Sivits restated the key insight of Nuremberg: that sane individuals have an innate ability to distinguish between right and wrong.

Unlike Sivits, most of the other soldiers who were involved in the prison scandal did not admit wrongdoing and maintained that they were acting responsibly because they were following orders. One of them, Pvt. 1st Class Lynndie R. England, presents a stark contrast to Sivits. On September 27, 2005, she was convicted of mistreatment of Iraqi prisoners at Abu Ghraib prison and was sentenced to three years in prison.

England, twenty-two, a chicken factory worker in civilian life, became a U.S. Army private who worked as a guard at the prison and was convicted of abuse based on actions such as holding a leash to a naked Iraqi prisoner's neck. She also posed for pictures laughing and joking while standing alongside groups of naked Iraqi prisoners whose hands were bound and who were piled in various formations. (It is a violation of Muslim custom and religion for men to be naked in the presence of women.)

England partly attributed her actions to her feelings for Charles Graner, the abuse ringleader and father of her child.[3] "I was embarrassed because I was used by Pvt. Graner; I didn't realize it at the time," she said. "I trusted him and I loved him."[4]

During a television interview before her trial, Private England justified what she did when she said:

> I mean, it [mistreatment of prisoners] got the information, and some of it was reliable. I mean, some of it was future attacks on the coalition forces. We don't feel like we were doing things that we weren't supposed to because we were told to do them. We think everything was justified because we were instructed to do this and to do that.[5]

In these remarks, England revealed her inability to evaluate torture and humiliation inflicted on prisoners as actions that are wrong, regardless of the benefits that might be derived from an unethical interrogation process. At her sentencing, England changed her evaluation of her conduct and admitted, "After the photos were released, I've heard that attacks were made on U.S. armed forces because of them. I apologize to coalition forces and all the families." England also apologized to "detainees, the families, America and all the soldiers."[6]

While we can gather from her remarks that Lynndie England eventually understood the wrongness of what she took part in, we are left to question whether she truly comprehends that members of the military are duty bound by ethical standards and that there can be no excuse for violating those standards. While Jeremy Sivits acknowledged that he had a responsibility to the Iraqi prisoners he was guarding and that he violated that responsibility, for quite a while Lynndie England was preoccupied with her relationship with Charles Graner and easily justified her misconduct based on following illegal orders. Her relationship should have been a secondary concern, and her military responsibilities should have been primary as she analyzed what she had done.

It is ironic that two of her lawyers also tried to evade this clear ethical conclusion. After charges against Lynndie England became known, during a May 2004 television interview with Katie Couric, Carl McGuire, one of Private England's attorneys, took her part:

> All through your military training you're told that you're not supposed to think, you're supposed to follow orders because, if you don't, people die. Someone could refuse an illegal order, but you're stuck in a hard situation. You are either going to refuse an order and end up at a court-martial, or follow an order and potentially end up at a court-martial. But either way, the enlisted personnel are told and taught not to interpret these orders, but to follow the orders of the people who are above them, and which is what our client did in this case.[7]

During the same interview, Giorgio Ra'Shadd, another of England's attorneys, also came to her defense, saying:

There were different and contradictory instructions given by the different intelligence operatives and the different personnel from military intelligence. [And] their commander, General Karpinski, wasn't allowed to get to them, and they weren't allowed to get out of that area.[8]

What neither of these counselors stated is that soldiers should stand for conscience and integrity rather than follow orders that will result in compromising principles.[9] Normal adults should recoil at the idea of torturing or humiliating a detainee. Yes, the information that detainees may have could be valuable, but intelligence gatherers need to use reasonable methods to get that information. The innate dignity of each human person requires that the person be treated with respect. The Geneva Conventions forbid the torture of prisoners, and this rule should be understood and followed by members of the armed forces who guard detainees.

Over the course of human history, people in communities have reached consensus about the morality of numerous kinds of actions. Reasoning together, people have come to agree that actions such as murder, rape, arson, stealing, child abuse, and driving while impaired are morally wrong actions. Society sees each of these actions as constituting a breach of the rights of innocent people.[10] There is no question that the people who commit such actions undermine their human dignity and deserve to be punished for their wrongdoing.

Members of the armed forces need to meet the moral requirements of military personnel. When individuals make the decision to join the military, they voluntarily take a significant step in determining how they want to spend an important part of their lives. This career move needs to be accompanied by thoughtful consideration of the moral aspects of being a soldier, sailor, marine, or member of the Air Force, Coast Guard, or Reserves.

Ordinarily, soldiers act ethically who follow orders and do their jobs. Occasionally, as with the military police at Abu Ghraib in November 2003, morality necessitates refusing orders. If soldiers refuse orders so as to do the morally right thing, they will bring honor to themselves and to the military, and they will not bring unnecessary harm to others. While it may seem expedient or beneficial to follow illegal orders, upon reflection, people should come to the realization that following illegal orders leads to injustice to others and personal disgrace.

The last time men were drafted for military service was during the Vietnam War; the draft ended in 1972, and women have never been drafted. As it stands today, the U.S. armed forces are made up of volunteers who enlist because they want to be part of the military. The Selective Service does require men to complete a draft registration form within thirty days of their eighteenth birthday, but most people do not think that compulsory military service will be reinstituted in the foreseeable future. It is surprising that volunteers for military service could exhibit the level of ignorance of the prison guards at Abu Ghraib, and the fact of this ignorance underscores the need for instruction in military ethics.

Exercise of Conscience

John J. Conley, SJ, follows natural law tradition when he credits philosopher Austin Fagothey with providing a well-reasoned definition of conscience:

> Austin Fagothey provides a definition of conscience typical of this [natural law] tradition: "Conscience may… be defined as the practical judgment of reason upon an individual act as good and to be performed, or as evil and to be avoided." This definition insists upon the intellectual dimension of conscience. Conscience emerges as the judgment of reason upon human action to be performed or shunned.[11]

As persons of conscience, humans can identify a subjective capacity to reason about what choices would be morally right or morally wrong as well as an ability to choose to follow one course or the other. Both law and experience affirm that sane adults are rational and free and consequently bear responsibility for their actions. Expressions such as "clear conscience" and "guilty conscience" have made their way into common parlance, reinforcing the idea that people know right from wrong and experience a loss of integrity when they fail to do what is required of them.

Frequently when people need to reach a decision of conscience they experience a conflict. The classic military case of being ordered to fire on civilians could constitute such a conflict. The person receiving this order would probably think, "I should do what I'm told; that's my job." Simultaneously, the person would also be thinking, "But these people are civilians, not enemy forces, and they should not be targeted." By applying the norm that the military should respect noncombatant immunity from direct attack to the situation at hand, members of the armed forces would reach the rational conclusion that the superior's order should be refused. Being in a situation in which one is pulled in two directions—between following orders and abiding by moral principles—represents an uncomfortable conflict. Conscience provides the mechanism for resolving the conflict satisfactorily.

Personal Integrity

Individuals who are committed to personal integrity live by sound moral principles, are upright, and can defend choices as morally correct. People whose lives reflect integrity are honest and can be counted on to do the right thing, no matter how much personal sacrifice is involved. In the military, people of integrity are brave and patriotic; they are also highly principled in the conduct of war.[12] A philosopher, R. M. Hare, writes insightfully of the temptation to surrender personal integrity by obeying illegal orders:

To get rid of one's moral problems on the shoulders of someone else—some political or military leader, some priest or commissar—is to be free of much worry; it is to exchange the tortured responsibility of the adult for the happy irresponsibility of the child; that is why so many have taken this course.[13]

Harkening back to the days of chivalry, men and women in uniform need to appreciate the ideals that accompany fighting the good fight and to reject as unworthy any inclination to compromise their principles.

Duties of Military Professionals

To be a member of the armed forces means to be required to fulfill the duties that go with that profession. A *duty* is the obligation to perform an action or actions demanded by one's humanity, state of life, and job or profession. Thus, military personnel who are part of a fighting force have a duty to fight in the battles in which their units are engaged. Military leaders likewise have a duty to implement strategies that will yield the greatest military gains at the cost of the least harm to their compatriots. The duties to engage in combat as well as to plan for successful combat are derived from the fact that soldiers and generals belong to the military profession. Civilians do not have comparable duties because military personnel are in a separate category and it is precisely from their identity as military professionals that their duties spring. It would be a mistake, however, to think that the duties of military professionals are limited to strategizing for war and war fighting. It is also the duty of soldiers and generals to conform their conduct and their planning to the moral limits imposed by the just war tradition. Even though, since Clausewitz, military might aimed at an efficient and speedy victory has been at the forefront of discussions about waging war, the duty to limit the horrors of war so as to protect from harm those not involved in the fighting remains.

Post-Conventional Behavior

As people mature physically and emotionally they also have opportunities to develop ethically. Three-year-olds do not take their siblings' toys because they do not want to get punished. Ideally, twenty-three-year-olds do not take things that do not belong to them because they respect their neighbor's right to private property, because they value law-abiding communities, and because they esteem themselves and do not want to compromise their integrity by stealing. If this is their motivation, they have grown significantly beyond the moral sensitivity of three-year-olds.

The late Lawrence Kohlberg, a professor of psychology at Harvard University, studied the process of moral development and proposed a stage theory that describes how ethical development takes place. Stages that are relevant to members of the armed forces are the conventional and post-conventional stages.

Stage 4 is a conventional level of moral development and is characterized by support for the law precisely because it is the law. Individuals who operate at stage 4 experience a sense of shared membership in a group and they try to be cooperative citizens. The attitude toward the law is one of obedience and respect. The law should be kept because it keeps order in society. By extension, in the military, orders should be obeyed; they should not be questioned or disobeyed.[14]

The post-conventional level of moral development, stages 5 and 6, is ordinarily not attained before age twenty, and relatively few adults achieve it. Stage 5 reasoning typifies the political philosophy of the United States: the value of consensus is affirmed, and a choice is made to uphold the political consensus, regardless of its content. Stage 5 thinking understands that patriotic Americans pay their taxes because the amount and the nation's expenditures are determined by a democratic process. Both responsibility to participate in representative government and willingness to go along with the compromises reached in a pluralistic society are stressed at stage 5.[15]

The person who attains stage 6, the highest stage of development, is autonomous in moral reasoning and decides what ought to be done in light of the universal principle of justice. Principled thinking sometimes provides the rationale for separating oneself from the majority, causing one to go so far as to break the law, or refuse to follow a military order, or even oppose a government's decision to go to war.[16] Consider Martin Luther King Jr.'s testimony when he was jailed in Birmingham, Alabama, for civil disobedience:

> One who breaks an unjust law must do so openly. An individual who breaks the law that conscience tells him is unjust, and willingly accepts the penalty of imprisonment in order to arouse the conscience of the community over injustice is, in reality, expressing the highest respect for the law.[17]

As members of the armed forces carry out their responsibilities, they may refuse an order or refuse to continue fighting. If this happens, people are likely to criticize them and authorities are likely to punish them. According to Lawrence Kohlberg and Martin Luther King Jr., individuals whose refusal is based on conscience and sound analysis should be applauded, not punished, because they have achieved a high level of moral development.

Blind Obedience

There are people who argue that the military is structured in such a way that the only response to orders should be compliance. Commanders see a big picture and direct campaigns with overarching objectives in view. Subordinates need to obey commanders so as to maintain order and contribute appropriately to predetermined goals. In the military, divergence from established routines and order would lead to disorganization, which could result in the sabotaging of important missions as well as grave risk to one's peers.

A strong case can be made for blind obedience, that is, following orders and not questioning their merits. However, it can happen that a subordinate receives illegal or immoral orders. In such a case, subordinates should refuse orders because they violate the just war criteria and undermine both the war effort and personal integrity.

Hugh Thompson, the helicopter pilot who stopped the massacre at the village of My Lai in Vietnam, understood that illegal orders need to be disregarded and that soldiers have a moral obligation to see that immoral conduct is stopped:

> The thought was going through my mind and my [helicopter] crew's mind, how these people got in that ditch and after coming up with about three scenarios, one of them being an artillery hit them, you wipe that out of your mind 'cause every house in Vietnam, I think, has a bunker underneath it. If artillery was coming there, they would go to the bunker, they wouldn't go outside in the open area. Then I said, well, when artillery was coming, they were going to leave and a round caught them in the ditch while they were going for cover. I threw that one out of my mind. Then something just sunk into me that these people were marched into that ditch and murdered. That was the only explanation that I could come up with.[18]

Convinced that what he witnessed from his helicopter was the assassination of civilians, Hugh Thompson landed his craft and confronted the soldiers on the ground who were engaged in the annihilation of the population of My Lai. Thompson ordered them to stop and said that he and his crewmates would execute the U.S. soldiers carrying out the massacre unless they ceased shooting. His threat succeeded, and the carnage was finished. By his intervention, Hugh Thompson not only put a stop to the annihilation of civilians, his account also drives home the unmistakable point that illegal orders should be refused and the principle of noncombatant immunity respected.

Loyalty versus Integrity

Loyalty is a strong force that binds individuals to one another in groups and prompts willingness to sacrifice for the benefit of others. Loyalty enables people to move beyond narcissism and individualism so as to be concerned for others and motivated to act in their behalf. As a result of loyal connectedness, associations are formed and people experience the psychologically beneficial result of identifying with groups to which they belong.

In the military, loyalty functions as glue that holds peers together and that makes officers feel responsible to those they lead and soldiers feel responsive to their commanders. Loyalty is a good aspect of the military, but situations can arise in which the demands of loyalty collide with the demands of integrity. When this happens, how should a soldier respond?

This question makes us face the fact that we do not live in a perfect world and that, at times, hard choices must be made. The spirit of the just war tradition leads to the insight that personal integrity should come before loyalty. While a sailor's refusal to rock the boat will result in a temporary calm, this state of affairs will be short-lived and the distress that follows will be significant if, in acquiescing to an unethical order, the sailor violates military codes of conduct.

The principles at the heart of the *jus in bello*—namely, noncombatant immunity from direct attack and just intention in the conduct of war—need to be observed, regardless of the orders of a commander. Commanders do not have the authority to absolve subordinates of these requirements, no matter what the situation.

Let us return to My Lai. Fueled by anger and battle fatigue during the Vietnam War, the soldiers in Lieutenant Calley's platoon in 1968 were reluctant to disobey their commanding officer and refuse orders to fire on civilians. They abandoned their integrity when they fired on civilians, and they undermined the loyalty they may have mistakenly sought to uphold. By some estimates, up to five hundred civilians in the hamlet of My Lai were killed in one day, mowed down by soldiers who ignored the fact that the unarmed people were elderly men, women of all ages, and children as young as infants.[19] Ultimately, My Lai harmed the morale of the U.S. military and irreparably undermined the integrity of the U.S. soldiers who were involved.

Hugh Thompson, who intervened on behalf of civilians at My Lai, died on January 6, 2006. An obituary reads, "For years Mr. Thompson suffered snubs from those who considered him unpatriotic. He recalled a congressman saying that Mr. Thompson himself was the only serviceman who should be punished for My Lai."[20] The same obituary also related that over time the ethical value of Thompson's intervention came to be recognized:

> In 1998 the Army honored the three men [Thompson and the other two members of his helicopter crew] with the prestigious Soldier's Medal, the highest award for bravery not involving conflict with an enemy.
>
> "It was the ability to do the right thing even at the risk of their personal safety that guided these soldiers to do what they did," Army Maj. Gen. Michael Ackerman said at the 1998 ceremony. The three "set the standard for all soldiers to follow."[21]

Members of the armed forces sometimes ask what will happen to them if they disobey a commander and the commander retaliates. This, unfortunately, is a realistic possibility, and it forces members of the armed forces to calculate the importance of maintaining their integrity. Doing the morally right thing may result in punishment, but, in the end, ethics teaches that it is better to risk being unfairly punished than to compromise one's conscience.

First Criterion: *Jus in Bello*

Having considered what is involved in acting ethically in the military services, it is now appropriate to consider what individual military personnel need to realize as they carry out their assignments. The first criterion of the *jus in bello* states, Only right means may be employed in the conduct of war and only enemy combatants may be the targets of direct attack.[22]

Right means refers to military strategy as well as weaponry. It would be morally wrong for a member of the military to wear a disguise such as a clergyperson's distinctive garb in order to trick an enemy and gain an advantage. Therefore, individuals in the armed forces should wear uniforms; by so doing, these individuals are observing the right means dictated by the just war criteria. Likewise, it would be morally wrong to wage an attack upon an enemy force when that force is gathered in a place of worship. Throughout history combatants have respected the neutrality of sanctuaries and have considered them off limits for fighting.

As far as weapons are concerned, so-called conventional weapons are considered morally acceptable, while nonconventional weapons are deemed unacceptable. Nuclear, chemical, and biological weapons are categorized as nonconventional; all other armaments in the U.S. arsenal can legitimately be utilized to achieve military objectives.

There are several reasons that the use of nuclear weapons is considered immoral. Nuclear weapons date from 1945, when scientists demonstrated how to split the atom and unleash its power in a bomb. In the summer of 1945, the United States and the other Allied powers were at war with Japan. The Axis powers had been defeated in Europe, but the war in the Asian theatre dragged on. U.S. President Harry Truman decided to order that Hiroshima and Nagasaki, two cities in Japan, be bombed on August 5 and August 8 so as to force Japan's emperor to surrender. Truman's strategy was successful, and the Japanese surrendered unconditionally on August 14, 1945.

The atomic bombings by U.S. forces on those two occasions many years ago constitute the only times that nuclear weapons have been used in the conduct of war. Many people defend Truman's order to use the atomic bombs as morally acceptable because the devastation and enormous loss of life at Hiroshima and Nagasaki moved the Japanese leadership to surrender. If the Japanese had not surrendered, the thinking goes, hundreds of thousands of Allied forces would have died in a land invasion, as well as an incalculable number of Japanese, mainly military, but including many civilians, too. Essentially the justification came down to a numerical calculation, with the emphasis on sparing the lives of as many Allied military as possible.

A major problem with this calculation is that the long-established rule against targeting civilians was ignored. The problem with the use of nuclear weapons is that in all probability they cannot be used and the principle of noncombatant immunity upheld. Because this principle is an enduring feature of the just war tradition, many people think that it was ethically wrong to use the atomic bombs in 1945 and that it would be immoral ever to unleash nuclear weapons in the future.

It is possible to argue that tactical nuclear weapons, which have been developed in recent years, could be precisely targeted and used against enemy troops or installations. There are problems, however, with this line of thinking. If nuclear weapons were used by a nation state, the taboo against using this type of weapon would be violated. Once this line is crossed, warring parties would risk escalation to the use of more deadly nuclear weapons and more widespread annihilation. And whether nuclear weapons are limited tactical weapons or more powerful weapons, their destructive potential and radioactive aftereffects are incalculably greater than conventional weapons and cannot be estimated in advance. Thus, because harm to civilians who are not targeted cannot be ruled out and likely would be catastrophic, a ban against the use of nuclear weapons should remain in place.

Most nations do not possess nuclear weapons. At the height of the so-called arms race, in the 1970s and 1980s, there were close to fifty thousand nuclear weapons in existence. The vast majority of these weapons were controlled by the United States and the then Union of Soviet Socialist Republics, which has since split into several different sovereign nations. During the past few decades, the superpowers have reduced the number of nuclear weapons in their defense arsenals. At the same time, in opposition to international pressure, such nations as North Korea and Iran are alleged to be involved in the development of nuclear weapons, undermining the stability of the entire world.

According to the official Korean Central News Agency, on October 9, 2006, North Korea successfully conducted an underground test of a nuclear weapon. A few days later, on October 14, 2006, the United Nations Security Council condemned the test and imposed sanctions on North Korea, calling for it to return immediately to multilateral talks. The council unanimously adopted Resolution 1718 (2006), which prevents a range of goods from entering or leaving the Democratic People's Republic of Korea and imposes an asset freeze and travel ban on persons related to the nuclear weapon program. North Korean President Kim Jong il surprised world leaders when, on October 31, 2006, he agreed to participate in talks with South Korea, Japan, China, Russia, and the United States. Although no conditions were set regarding the substance of the talks, the hoped-for conclusion is that North Korea will abandon its nuclear program and become a peaceful neighbor to other Asian nations.

Individual members of the military who may at some future date be ordered to launch a nuclear weapon or fight on the ground with tactical nuclear weapons will face a momentous decision. The late Joseph Cardinal Bernardin, a leading member of the Catholic hierarchy in the United States, said that anyone ordered to execute a nuclear attack against a city should refuse to obey the order.[23]

Will that order ever again be given? No one knows for certain, because political and military leaders contend that they need to be able to threaten foes with nuclear attacks in order to deter those foes from initiating belligerent action. This fact leaves individual members of the armed forces at a decided disadvantage, because, if they are told to fire a nuclear weapon, it will mean that they will need to stand in opposition to the political-military establishment in order to do the right thing.

The other types of weapons that are condemned as immoral are chemical and biological weapons (CBW). Chemical weapons include lethal toxic chemicals in vapor or liquid form that, after inhalation, ingestion, or skin penetration, kill rapidly; toxins such as botulin, which kill those who inhale or ingest them; incapacitating chemical agents that are temporarily disabling, such as tear gas, or that cause skin blistering and damage to the eyes and/or the lungs, such as mustard gas, which is fatal in 2 percent of cases and may be permanently disabling to other victims; and any chemicals that, when placed in a water supply or applied to an agricultural area, have the capability of poisoning them.[24] Biological weapons include viruses, rickettsiae, bacteria, or fungi that can be disseminated into or over a large area and that can be expected to cause illness to members of a targeted population.[25]

The reasons why the use of chemical and biological weapons is considered immoral are that opponents cannot defend themselves against CBW, and that these weapons are unpredictable and could boomerang and kill one's own comrades. One of the presuppositions underlying the just war criteria is that those who fight for a defensible goal ought to engage in a fair fight. Since one cannot defend against CBW, the possibility of a fair fight does not exist, thereby precluding the use of these weapons. Additionally, the unique and horrific qualities of CBW have led to a dread of their being used in military combat or intentionally or accidentally against civilians.

This dread has found expression in agreements among nations not to use CBW. A treaty banning the use of toxins and biological warfare drawn up at the Geneva Disarmament Conference in 1971 was approved by the United Nations General Assembly on December 16, 1971, and signed by the United States and seventy other countries on April 10, 1972. The U.S. Senate ratified this treaty and the 1925 Geneva Protocol on December 16, 1974. The 1972 Convention stated:

> Each State Party to this Convention undertakes never in any circumstances to develop, produce, stockpile or otherwise acquire or retain:
> (1) Microbial or other biological agents, or toxins whatever their origin or method of production, of types or in quantities that have no justification for prophylactic, protective or other peaceful purposes;
> (2) Weapons, equipment or means of delivery designed to use such agents or toxins for hostile purposes or in armed conflict.[26]

At a conference in Paris, France, in January 1989, 149 states discussed strengthening the authority of the 1925 Geneva Protocol with the intention of preventing any use of chemical weapons by completely eliminating them. These nations, of which the United States was one, called for a global ban that would prohibit the production of chemical and biological weapons and mandate the destruction of existent weapons under effective international control.[27] This initiative was acted on when, on January 14, 1993, more than 120 nations, including the United States, signed a treaty called the Chemical Weapons Convention. This treaty is considered unique because it is global, includes sanctions against nonsignatory nations, and establishes the most complex verification system ever conceived to monitor compliance. Given the cooperation of so many nations and their consensus against possession or use of CBW, it is obvious that the use of these weapons would not be in accordance with the just war criteria.

The second half of the criterion under discussion states that only enemy combatants may be the targets of direct attack. This means that members of the armed forces should engage only their counterparts on the enemy side. Accordingly, civilians should be respected and not targeted. As the weapons of conventional warfare became more deadly and capable of extensive death and destruction, both within and beyond the site of battle, a distinction was introduced regarding collateral damage. By "collateral damage" is meant loss of life and property that is unintended and cannot be controlled as military maneuvers unfold. As long as every reasonable effort is made to minimize civilian casualties, and these casualties comprise a very small number alongside the number of enemy military who are killed, the deaths of civilians in wartime can be morally tolerated according to the logic of collateral damage. A key ethical aspect of this notion is that the direct intention is to kill military targets; civilians are not targeted and only indirectly get caught up in the carnage because they have the misfortune of being in the wrong place at the wrong time. This reasoning is in accord with the principle of the double effect, which was explained by Saint Thomas Aquinas and which became an important component of just war thinking.

Knowing that only enemy combatants may be the targets of direct attack requires that members of the armed forces also acknowledge that various categories of people, many of whom wear the enemy uniform, should not be attacked. These categories include prisoners of war, wounded enemy combat forces and medics who treat them, retreating enemy forces, and detainees, whether detained based on political, military, or ideological factors. The reasons these categories of opponents should not be attacked are that they are not engaged in offensive actions, they are injured and present no threat, or they are imprisoned and are incapable of inflicting harm. Drafters of the Geneva Conventions and similar accords sought to obtain humane treatment for military personnel in these types of situations so as to restrict combat to able warriors and bring humanitarian considerations to bear on those who are no longer involved in belligerent activities.

Second Criterion: *Jus in Bello*

The second *jus in bello* criterion that military forces must adhere to is this statement: As war progresses, a just intention should be evident in the strategy of war. This rule is meant to make individual members of the armed forces realize that in most wars neither side is totally right or totally wrong. Therefore, just as the soldiers on one side believe in the righteousness of their cause, so, probably, do the combatants on the other side, and neither side is above reproach. If opponents internalize the essence of this criterion, they will be less inclined to inflict pain and humiliation when they are at a military advantage. They will also resist the temptation to demonize their opponents, denying that those who are enemies are also humans. Crimes such as rape, plunder, destruction of property, and assassination of retreating forces or prisoners of war will not be features of the final days of the war effort. There may even be a sense of empathy according to which the enemy is seen as another human being who is caught up in a dreadful enterprise and is trying to conduct himself bravely.

Conclusion

Within any discussion of the moral limits on warfare, a difficult question arises: What happens when the other side doesn't play by the rules? There are two possible answers to this question:

First, the rules are the rules and observing the just war criteria enables armed forces to see themselves as noble warriors; they should continue to do the right thing, regardless of an enemy's treachery.

Second, when the enemy violates the rules of war it is acceptable for the other side to abandon these rules and not consider themselves required to observe the limits of the laws of war.

In light of our discussions of conscience, integrity, principled behavior, and the *jus in bello* criteria, it should be obvious that the way to prevent combat from becoming barbaric is to observe the limits required by international law and the just war tradition. If the enemy disregards the criteria and abandons restraint, this undoubtedly puts opponents at a disadvantage. Opponents can respond by continuing to fight with honor, or they can disregard the rules and limits of warfare.

No armed force wants to be faced with such a choice, because both the lives and the honor of combatants are on the line. However, it needs to be noted that, if there is anything as valuable as life itself, it is a person's honor and the strength of a good conscience. These ideals, proclaimed by military leaders, require combatants to continue to observe the rules of war so as not to sink to the depths of depravity embraced by combatants who do not observe the rules. However, making these general guidelines specific to any particular instance of armed conflict is the responsibility of military leadership and takes form in the so-called rules of engagement. Rules of engagement are formulated with the best interests of the members of the armed forces in mind. They are the subject of chapter 3.

Discussion Questions

1. Why do you think the average citizen in the United States tends to support a president's decision to go to war?
2. Contrast remarks made by Jeremy Sivits and Lynndie England, stating which individual showed more moral insight and reflecting on why.
3. What is conscience? How should conscience function on a battlefield?
4. What guides moral behavior at stage 6 of Lawrence Kohlberg's schema? Why does stage 6 represent the highest degree of moral development?
5. What should be more important to members of the armed forces, loyalty or integrity? Why?
6. Should members of the armed forces obey orders to use nuclear, chemical, or biological weapons? Why or why not?
7. What is meant by "collateral damage"? What steps should be taken to minimize collateral damage? Why?
8. When one side in combat does not observe the rules of war, how should the other side respond?

Case Study

The context of this situation is that the United States is waging a war against terror in a Middle Eastern nation and the war is going poorly. The main obstacles to establishing stability in the nation are frequent car bombings and unpredictable attacks by insurgents against U.S. forces.

The members of one U.S. company, a support group entrusted with transporting matériel throughout the combat zone, have been hit hard; six members have been killed and two have suffered catastrophic injuries. This company's tour has been extended and there are many signs of low morale.

The company's commander is concerned about the morale of her troops; she also pays close attention to the U.S. media, monitoring it via the Internet. The commander is especially angry about the fact that the media is becoming increasingly critical of the war effort.

The commander receives an advisory from Centcom that an embedded reporter is being assigned to her unit. Because of her familiarity with war reporting, she recognizes the reporter as a strong critic of the war effort. She fears that this reporter will be a negative influence on her troops and that the reporter's bias will translate into even lower morale, making her job that much more difficult.

The commander schedules a meeting with a prominent member of her unit. She tells him to arrange an accident in which the reporter will be seriously injured, forcing him to return to the United States for medical treatment.

1. What should the soldier do who is ordered to stage the accident? Why?
2. Evaluate the motives and directions of the commander.
3. Discuss the importance of war reporting and efforts to portray a war in a good light.

CHAPTER THREE
RULES OF ENGAGEMENT

The topics "the just war tradition" and "the good soldier" are broad and general, providing information and insight, but they fall short of giving specific directions to military personnel who are on the ground fighting a war on terror such as the one the United States embarked on following 9/11, which entails military action in Afghanistan and Iraq.

The war against terrorism and terrorists differs from traditional types of warfare as we have come to understand these traditional types. There is virtually no battlefield combat in the war on terror. Instead, sophisticated weapons such as laser-guided bombs can be deployed from remote locations to destroy distant targets. In such scenarios, those deploying the bombs focus on geographic coordinates and are far removed from the devastating results. On the other hand, when U.S. soldiers on the ground are searching out enemy forces, or suspected terrorists, or warring insurgents, they are often in cities or villages, and they employ guerrilla-like tactics. Since the enemy is a terrorist or an insurgent, he or she does not wear a uniform and is not easily distinguished from civilians. Guerrilla warfare calls for locating, disarming, capturing, or killing specific individuals or groups who frequently are interspersed among civilians. Guerrilla warfare also requires that troops defend themselves from attacks by hard-to-identify hostile forces. In both types of circumstances, offensive and defensive, U.S. armed forces must attempt to remove civilians from harm's way or to protect civilians while pursuing the enemy. This task can be impossibly difficult in environments wherein soldiers are unsure if people are civilians or enemy forces. "When should I shoot?" "Whom should I target?" "When should I hold fire?" "How am I to recognize hostile forces when I encounter them?" Crucially important questions such as these preoccupy members of the armed forces. These questions demand clear and precise answers. Directions to military personnel about how to carry out their duties in the particular circumstances of a given war are contained in rules of engagement. One feature of rules of engagement is that their purpose is to give soldiers a fighting chance against enemies who do not observe rules.

Dangerous situations often demand split-second decisions, and life or death hangs in the balance. On these occasions of extreme duress, when confronted by a hostile, threatening opponent, members of the armed forces have been taught that they can use necessary and appropriate force in self-defense. Beyond this, they need instructions about how to conduct operations or respond to attacks that occur in the types of situations they typically encounter. Rules of engagement (ROE), handed down by officers to subordinates, provide information about how force is to be used against a hostile force in a context of self-defense or carrying out a mission. Rules of engagement are formulated in advance of armed confrontations; they prescribe what actions are to be taken in various predictable scenarios. Tailoring rules to specific situations is an important aspect of formulating them. Accordingly,

> in addition to a typically large set of standing orders, military personnel will be given additional rules of engagement before performing any mission or military operation. These can cover circumstances such as how to retaliate after an attack, how to treat captured targets, which territories the soldier is bound to fight into, and how force should be used during the operation.[1]

Because those who are writing rules of engagement cannot foresee all possible future circumstances, rules may allow for the use of discretion on the part of either superior officers or troops on the ground. If this is the case, those who order or exercise means beyond those prescribed bear the burden of justifying their decisions.

Rules of engagement are designed to direct that the proper amount of force to accomplish a mission be used, while unnecessary force is avoided. U.S. forces who are on duty during military attacks against the United States and during military operations outside the United States receive rules of engagement. These rules function as a management tool that attempts to ensure that military tactics conform to the political goals of a military operation while giving the armed forces practical guidance in defending themselves.

The U.S. Department of Defense defines rules of engagement as "directives issued by competent military authority which delineate the circumstances and limitations under which United States forces will initiate and/or continue combat engagement with other forces encountered."[2]

Scott Sagan describes two general categories of rules of engagement:

> First, many ROE documents describe a set of military actions that can be taken at the discretion of a commander under certain specified circumstances *unless* explicitly negated by new orders from higher authorities. Second, ROE documents may also spell out military activities that can be taken by a commander only *if* explicitly authorized at some later point by a higher command decision. The first category of directives has been called "command by negation" provisions; the second set of directives constitutes "positive command" ROE provisions. Most rules of engagement documents contain a mixture of both these command elements.[3]

A basic principle learned by members of the armed forces is that they are justified in using armed force in self-defense. The person being attacked needs to determine what response is necessary and proportionate, and the rules of engagement under which he or she operates spell out what actions can be taken. A hostile action by a foe or probable hostile intent toward a member of the armed forces occasion the necessity to respond with appropriate force. A judgment must be made in an instant that the force used to counter a probable attack is reasonable in intensity and magnitude, given the threat that is anticipated.

Rules of Engagement

Just as action may be called for by rules of engagement, so is restraint encouraged. Those who fight our wars need to understand the difference between mere harassment by a foe and an enemy's threatened hostile act. The directions contained in rules of engagement should prepare soldiers to make this type of distinction. A genuinely hostile act calls for aggressive defense, while a merely harassing action should not be answered with lethal force.

An example of how formulating rules of engagement took shape in new circumstances post–9/11 was given by Gen. Richard Myers, USAF. Speaking before Congress, he referred to a situation in which the United States might again be attacked from the sky, stating that in the future there would be a decisive military counterattack. As you will recall, on the morning of September 11, 2001, four hijacked commercial airplanes were not intercepted by the U.S. Air Force, and three hit their intended targets.

> We now have a mature plan to protect against future airborne attacks originating from inside the continental United States. This includes air assets postured to respond—Operation NOBLE EAGLE, fully developed Rules of Engagement, and improved coordination with the FAA.[4]

Thus, General Myers is disclosing that designated Air Force personnel have received orders about how to proceed in the future to stop a plane that poses a threat to a building or other target. While Myers assured Congress that a plan was in place, he did not divulge the particulars of the plan for the obvious reason that the general does not want to inform enemies of the United States about classified military strategies.

Two types of practical problems are associated with rules of engagement. In the first instance, excessively strict rules can so limit a field commander that the commander cannot direct enough force against an enemy to accomplish a mission. Political input from outside the military chain of command is often blamed for constricting military operations and preventing field commanders from accomplishing their objectives.

In contrast to strict rules of engagement, loose rules of engagement can result in overzealous use of force that can bring about a tactical military advantage while infuriating an enemy, thus causing an escalation in violence that undermines the political objectives of a military campaign. Thus, those who write rules of engagement are mindful of striking a balance between concern for the armed forces who need to defend themselves and regard for the overall mission in which the forces are deployed.

Rules of Engagement in Afghanistan and Iraq

As we will see in this section of the chapter, U.S. forces in Iraq and Afghanistan have received criticism because some of their actions have caused harm to Iraqi civilians, many of whom were in vehicles that did not stop at checkpoints; because of friendly fire casualties; and because of using deadly force against wounded Iraqis. The criticism has been accompanied by two questions:

1. Under what rules of engagement are U.S. forces operating?
2. What strategies are in place to prevent injuring or killing innocent civilians?

These are pertinent questions, but they are not easily answered. In respect to disclosing the rules of engagement under which U.S. forces operate, military leaders refuse to divulge this information. Their reasoning is obvious: any well-publicized rules of engagement would immediately be used by insurgent killers to create more death and destruction. The rules are meant to protect U.S. military personnel as well as civilians,[5] but, given the chaos of war, even the most thorough planning can result in civilian casualties and hostility directed against the United States.

In respect to how the rules of engagement were formulated for the military circumstances of patrolling roads in Iraq,

[A] military spokesman in Baghdad said the rules of engagement were written and issued by senior commanders in the 150,000-member American force here, and submitted for higher approval by the United States Central Command, which controls American military activities across the Middle East. The rules are passed down the chain of command, and thoroughly explained to every soldier operating a checkpoint or manning weapons in any vehicles in a convoy.

Because the rules are intended to protect soldiers coming under immediate attack, no telephone or radio calls to higher command are required before soldiers may put them into effect. "Rules of engagement are standing orders," he said. "These are briefed all the way down to the lowest level."

"Everybody knows what they are," he said. "They are automatic."[6]

The second question regarding strategies to prevent civilian injuries and deaths points to the vulnerable position in which civilians find themselves when a war against terrorists and insurgents is fought in their midst. Over and over again U.S. military leaders assure Iraqi civilians that civilians will never be targeted intentionally. However, these civilians need to understand that since the United States and its coalition partners[7] fight enemies who do not wear uniforms, mistakes can be made. Therefore, civilians need to be cautious and well informed about how to conduct themselves in dangerous places. Regarding checkpoints, civilians should know how they are expected to behave and what will be interpreted by soldiers as noncompliant behavior. Better signs, better use of the local media to provide pertinent information, and effective education and advertising should be used to accomplish this goal. The responsibility for this educational effort rests with the United States and the coalition forces since they are carrying out the campaign against terrorists and insurgents.

In the first half of 2006, in response to an effort initiated by Lt. Gen. Peter W. Chiarelli, the number two U.S. officer in Iraq, new measures intended to lessen the chances for violent confrontations and, consequently, collateral civilian deaths were put in place. Strategies involved include a delay in firing warning shots by requiring signs, hand signals, strobe lights, and even lasers in order to do all possible to facilitate civilian drivers seeing soldiers clearly, particularly at night. Since this new initiative was undertaken, "the number of Iraqi civilians killed at checkpoints, roadblocks or along convoys has dropped to an average of one per week." This number is down from an average of "one Iraqi civilian [killed] every day...by coalition forces during 2005."[8]

Improvised Explosive Devices and Car Bombs

Improvised explosive devices (IEDs) are a source of constant danger to U.S. troops who carry out operations in the urban and rural areas of Iraq. An IED

> can be almost anything with any type of material and initiator. It is a "homemade" device that is designed to cause death or injury by using explosives alone or in combination with toxic chemicals, biological toxins, or radiological material. IEDs can be produced in varying sizes, functioning methods, containers, and delivery methods. IEDs can utilize commercial or military explosives, homemade explosives, or military ordnance and ordnance components.[9]

IEDs can appear as charges laid in or alongside roads, or can be fillers for suicide bombers' cars and vests, or even be bombs used against airplanes. Garden hoses can be filled with explosives and laid across roadways. The delivery method can be a remote control timer made using an alarm clock, a cell phone, or some other easily obtained electronic device, or a person can detonate an IED and die in the process. To date, there is no record of Iraqi insurgents having used chemical or biological toxins or nuclear material in the explosive devices used to harm or kill U.S. and coalition troops or Iraqis who belong to different religious or political factions. However, conventional explosives have been used with devastating consequences.

> Improvised explosive devices, or IEDs, killed 302 U.S.
> troops between Jan. 1 and Oct. 7, [2005] compared with
> 165 in the same period of 2004, according to Iraq
> Coalition Casualty Count, an Internet site with statistics
> based on official U.S. casualty reports.[10]

In the first three years of the war in Iraq, one-third of all U.S. and coalition casualties have been caused by IEDs. Because of excellent medical care, wounded troops have very good chances for survival, so that thousands of men and women who have survived attacks from IEDs are struggling to recover from a wide range of disabling injuries.

One of the weapons most frequently used by Iraqi insurgents to destabilize Iraq and undermine efforts to achieve stability is the car bomb; in some cases the drivers die in the explosions and, in others, the car bombs are detonated by remote control. "In total, for the year from the handover of sovereignty on June 28, 2004, until June 22, 2005, there were at least 479 car bombs, killing 2,174 people and wounding 5,520."[11] Given the frequency of car bombings in Iraq, U.S. and coalition forces follow rules of engagement that try to prevent suspect vehicles from reaching their targets while also trying to keep the troops from being killed in explosions. The means designed to achieve this objective is the checkpoint, at which soldiers examine cars and other vehicles before clearing them to proceed. At checkpoints cars must stop and be examined before they are allowed to continue on their way. Drivers learn that they should stop by reading posted road signs that contain instructions, hand signals from troops at the checkpoint, shouted commands, and, finally, warning gun shots into the air. If, in spite of all these warnings, drivers do not stop, soldiers may open fire, killing some or all occupants of the vehicle. When mistakes are made, it is usually nearly impossible to determine exactly what steps were taken to make a vehicle stop and why it did not stop. There is also no commensurate way to make amends for the injuries and/or loss of life.

Civilian Casualties: Some Tragic Cases

The Amnesty International Web site details one incident of civilian casualties at a checkpoint. There have been countless others.

> March 31, 2003: Soldiers with the U.S. Army's 3rd Infantry Division killed seven women and children when they opened fire on an unidentified four-wheel drive vehicle as it approached a U.S. checkpoint near al-Najaf. According to a Pentagon spokesman, initial reports indicated that "the soldiers responded in accordance with the rules of engagement to protect themselves." However, this does not appear to be consistent with the version reported in the *Washington Post*, which indicated that the officer in command at the scene believed at the time that no warning shots were fired. It asserts that the officer roared at the platoon leader, "You just [expletive] killed a family because you didn't fire a warning shot soon enough!" The U.S. authorities said they were investigating the incident.[12]

When there is a highly publicized civilian casualty, the soldiers involved and the rules under which they operate receive a great deal of scrutiny. A case in point involves the killing on March 4, 2005, of an escort to a freed hostage, the Italian journalist Giuliana Sgrena. Details are contained in the following account:

> ROME—An Italian journalist was injured when a U.S. armored vehicle mistakenly fired on her car after she was released from her captors in Iraq. One Italian secret service agent was killed in the shooting, and another was injured, the reports said.
>
> The Apcom and ANSA news agencies said that Giuliana Sgrena, a reporter for the communist daily *Il Manifesto*, was in a hospital in Iraq with a shoulder

injury. The shooting occurred at a roadblock while the cars were heading to the airport.[13]

The inadvertent killing of Canadian military forces in April 2002 during the campaign against the Taliban in Afghanistan presents yet another example of a mistaken use of force, with tragic consequences.

> KABUL, Afghanistan—Four Canadian soldiers were killed in southern Afghanistan early today when a U.S. warplane mistakenly bombed them during a military exercise, prompting anguished demands for answers in Canada as the country mourned the first combat fatalities among its forces in a half-century.
>
> At least one U.S. Air National Guard pilot flying an F-16 fighter on patrol passed over the Canadian troops near the southern city of Kandahar, apparently unaware that a nighttime live-fire training drill was underway, military officials said. The pilot mistakenly thought he was under attack and dropped one or two 500-pound laser-guided bombs, killing the four soldiers and injuring eight other Canadians.[14]

One of the most controversial episodes involving the U.S. military and the specifics of their rules of engagement occurred following the killing of a wounded Iraqi in a mosque in Fallujah in November 2004. The case is described as follows:

> Images of the incident, captured Saturday on videotape by Kevin Sites, a freelance correspondent working for NBC News who is embedded with a Marine unit, were broadcast last night on several news networks. The videotape shows a squad of Marines entering the building and seeing several Iraqis lying against a wall, either dead or gravely wounded. One Marine shouts something about one Iraqi feigning death. The Marine then shoots the man in the head.[15]

These four cases, in which members of the U.S. military killed civilians, coalition forces, or wounded enemy forces, point to what can happen in wartime. It is understandable that members of the armed forces, faced with IEDs and car bombs on a daily basis, can feel threatened even when there is no threat and might respond by unwarranted killing so as to defend themselves. Since the military is supposed to do battle only against the enemy, the question of what went wrong, leading to the deaths of people who should not have been killed, is inevitably asked. A frequent answer, that the rules of engagement allowed for the action, illustrates that rules of engagement are frequently defended after the fact.

Justifications by military officials are given in response to three of the four instances recounted. In respect to soldiers or marines at checkpoints who fire on cars that do not heed orders to stop, U.S. military officials take for granted the right of armed forces to fire on vehicles that do not follow orders. This is implicit in a relevant press release from Centcom:

> At about 11:00 p.m., (on May 29, 2003) a vehicle moving at an estimated 40 mph tried to drive through a well-established and well-lit checkpoint guarded by Coalition soldiers and three tanks. Soldiers fired numerous warning shots but the vehicle continued onward, forcing soldiers on the ground to jump out of the way. The soldiers then fired at it with a tank-mounted machine gun, killing two civilians inside the vehicle.
>
> Two other civilians in the vehicle were injured and taken to the Samarra Hospital.[16]

The case of the wounded Italian journalist, Giuliana Sgrena, and her escort who was fatally shot received worldwide attention. While regret was expressed about the unfortunate death of the escort and the injury to Sgrena, U.S. military officials defended the action of the troops who shot at the vehicle. By so doing, these officials put forward the ethical judgment that the military personnel involved in the shooting acted legally and honorably, and they thus sent a message to other soldiers at other checkpoints to use force upon perceived provocation rather than put themselves at risk. Needless to say, Italian officials and many commentators throughout the world disagreed with U.S. rationale.

> The U.S. report absolved of all blame the American troops who shot and killed Nicola Calipari at a checkpoint near Baghdad International Airport and injured a released Italian journalist hostage, Giuliana Sgrena, who was traveling with him. The report on the findings of an investigation into the incident said the troops had followed the rules of engagement and no disciplinary action should be taken against them....
>
> The U.S. report said the car in which Calipari and Sgrena, plus another agent as driver, approached the checkpoint at high speed (50 mph) and failed to slow down in response to warning signals—shouts, a powerful spotlight, and warning shots fired in the air. Instead of stopping, the car increased speed, the report said, so the soldiers opened fire, ostensibly to disable the vehicle— except that Calipari was killed and Sgrena injured.[17]

Friendly fire deaths have occurred frequently in recent wars and, following these episodes, deciding whether or not action should be taken against those who fire in error is a major issue. In regard to the Canadian soldiers killed in Afghanistan in 2002, U.S. and Canadian authorities conducted a joint inquiry into the incident, finding those who fired guilty of misconduct.

Findings of Board of Inquiry

> Two Boards of Inquiry, one Canadian and one American, were held simultaneously. The two boards shared personnel and information. Canadian Brigadier-General M.J. Dumais was specialist advisor to the Canadian board and co-chair of the American board. The findings of the four-member Canadian Tarnak Farm Board of Inquiry, chaired by General Maurice Baril, were released on June 28th, 2002. The Board found that the Canadian troops engaged in the night

live-fire exercise had conducted their operations as authorized and in accordance with the established range procedures for the types of weapons fire. The Board concluded that the American F-16 pilots contravened established procedures and were the cause of the incident.

Disposition

On September 11, 2002, U.S. pilots, Majors Harry Schmidt and William Umbach were officially charged with 4 counts of negligent manslaughter, 8 counts of aggravated assault, and 1 count of dereliction of duty. On July 6, 2004 U.S. Lt.-Gen. Bruce Carlson found Schmidt guilty of dereliction of duty in what the U.S. military calls a "non-judicial hearing" before a senior officer. He was given thirty days of house arrest. Umbach was reprimanded for leadership failures and allowed to retire.

This was the most serious case of fratricide or friendly fire to have been experienced by the Canadian Forces (CF) in Coalition operations since the Korean War.[18]

The final incident noted concerned the shooting of a wounded Iraqi in a mosque. Because a reporter recorded this horrible event on tape and it was shown on news broadcasts all over the world, it generated a great deal of comment. Was the soldier in danger from the wounded man and did he act reasonably? At the time of the shooting, accounts were rife about booby-trapped injured and dead Iraqis: when they were touched, IEDs went off, killing the troops who sought to treat or move them. Or, did the soldier transgress ethical boundaries by his actions, and should he be punished? After all, rules of engagement require that an enemy display hostile intent before being attacked,[19] and, in conjunction with the Geneva Conventions, wounded persons are to be treated humanely. The U.S. military evaluated the case and ruled in favor of the marine:

The investigation into a controversial shooting of a wounded Iraqi by a U.S. Marine has ended with a determination the Marine acted in self-defense.

The Marines announced no charges would be filed in the incident last November in which a Camp Pendleton infantryman shot a wounded Iraqi insurgent following a firefight around a mosque in the city of Fallujah.

The incident was captured on video by a reporter accompanying the patrol from Pendleton's 1st Marine Regiment and raised allegations the shooting violated the laws of war.

The Marines said Maj. Gen. Richard Natonski, commander of the 1st Marine Division, reviewed the incident and determined the unidentified Marine acted within his right to self-defense.

The Marine told investigators he had, in fact, killed three wounded Iraqi fighters he feared still posed a threat to his unit.

Natonski reportedly gave serious consideration to intelligence reports that said injured insurgents in Fallujah had feigned surrender and then attacked American troops as they approached.[20]

Pending Cases of Wrongful Conduct Entailing Civilian Deaths

At this writing, several cases involving deaths to Iraqi civilians at the hands of U.S. military personnel are being investigated. In most cases the name of the location in which the alleged illegal actions occurred is used to identify the case.

Haditha, Iraq. Members of Kilo Company, 3rd Battalion, First Marines, who were fighting in Haditha on November 19, 2005, were hit by an IED, and one of them was killed. It is alleged that in retaliation some marines (three or four) responded out of anger and killed to avenge their comrade's death, entering two or three houses and killing civilians. Approximately twenty-four men, women, and children died as a result, and the killings have led to an investigation, the detaining of marines who await trial, and a call by military authorities for additional ethics training for troops on the ground. (Defenders of the accused marines said that troops were acting in accordance with rules of engagement when they entered houses where marines thought insurgents were hiding and, in order to disable hostile forces, the marines sprayed the rooms with bullets before going into them.)

In regard to the possibility that marines intentionally killed civilians at Haditha, Maj. Gen. William Caldwell, spokesman for the Multinational Force-Iraq, told a Baghdad news briefing that the training was designed to reinforce what troops learned before coming to Iraq. "It will focus on 'values and looking at the legal, moral and ethical standards that every one of us in uniform here, as guests of the Iraqi government, need to adhere to,' he said."[21]

Hamdania, Iraq. It is alleged that a fifty-two-year-old disabled Iraqi was killed on April 26, 2006, in Hamdania, west of Baghdad, by U.S. troops and that his killing was unwarranted and illegal. Seven marines and a Navy corpsman were charged with premeditated murder in this man's death and are being held in individual cells at Camp Pendleton, California. According to media reports, an unidentified

> senior Pentagon official with direct knowledge of the investigation said evidence so far indicates troops entered the town in search of an insurgent and, failing to find him, grabbed an unarmed man from his home and shot him. After the killing, the troops planted a shovel and an AK-47 rifle at the scene to make it appear the man was trying to plant an explosive device, said the official, who spoke on condition of anonymity because he is not authorized to discuss the matter publicly.[22]

Obviously, there is no way rules of engagement could justify conduct such as that described by the senior Pentagon official just quoted.

The eight troops who are in custody have retained attorneys and are at the beginning of a process that could end in military court martial.

Salahuddin Province. A complicated case that relates to possibly illegal rules of engagement is centered in Iraq's Salahuddin Province. Illegal rules of engagement are directions given to troops by superiors that clearly violate the rules of war; they should not be followed.

On May 9, 2006, U.S. troops carried out a raid against what was believed to be an al-Qaeda training camp on an island in a canal in northern Salahuddin province. When the U.S. soldiers reached the island, they located three men who were using two women and a toddler as shields. After separating the men from their human shields, the U.S. soldiers killed the men. Contradictions emerge from different sources that comment about why the soldiers killed the men. An attorney for one soldier says that the troops were under orders to kill all military-age males and that their actions were within their rules of engagement. U.S. military authorities, who charged the soldiers with murder and other offenses, do not accept a defense based on purported rules of engagement because the captives who were killed posed no danger to the soldiers. To be determined is the truth of the U.S. soldier's contention that, once in custody, the captives, as they were being restrained, attacked the soldiers, becoming a threat. In the context of this chapter, lessons from Salahuddin province are that rules of engagement are invalid if they order the killing of alleged enemy forces who are in custody and pose no threat; superiors should not issue such orders and subordinates should not follow them.[23]

Responsibility of Commanders

Troops on the ground do not have much time to react when they are in real or perceived danger. It is at times like these that their training takes over and they react according to their training. Soldiers follow orders; those who issue the orders bear more responsibility than those who execute them. This is the reason that commanding officers need to get rules of engagement right. Just as it is a matter of life and death for armed forces personnel, so it is also a matter of honor or dishonor for individual military personnel, commanding officers, and the armed forces as a whole. Troops on the ground will live with the consequences of their choices for the rest of their lives, and a burdened conscience is a terrible weight to carry. And, it goes without saying that if a life is taken in error, that wrong can never be righted.

Rules of Engagement and the Just War Criteria

When military leaders make plans regarding how troops are to defend themselves against hostile forces, these leaders are constrained by the laws of war. The laws of war, as we have seen, are expressed in general terms in the just war criteria. Military commanders who write rules of engagement and who communicate these rules to troops on the ground do so in order to protect the troops and advance a nation's mission. Rules of engagement set boundaries for military personnel and, if they are prudent and practical, the rules will avoid the pitfalls of overreaction and underreaction.[24] The rules will also conform to the letter and spirit of the just war tradition, thus lessening the possibility of intemperate actions that result in horrific consequences. Obviously, any order to kill civilians directly or to kill enemies who pose no danger would be an illegal order and should not be issued or followed. While it will never be possible for drafters of rules of engagement to eliminate the vulnerability of troops in the situations they face in places like Iraq, practical guidance for dangerous situations represents the best strategy to protect the troops without compromising the integrity of the mission.

It is imperative that commanding officers who write rules of engagement understand the reasons for, and limits to, those actions they endorse. In this regard, Maj. D. B. Hall, USMC, writes:

The right of self-defense contains the caveats of necessity and proportionality. Necessity exists when a hostile act has been committed or hostile intent has been exhibited. The law of proportionality requires that any necessary use of force be reasonable in intensity, duration, and magnitude, based on all facts known to the commander at the time. [Operational Law Handbook, 8-20] ROE also restricts the operational concepts of retaliation and pursuit. In other words, the use of force must be immediate, of short duration, and in the right proportion to the threat. These two qualifiers on the use of force, whether lethal or non-lethal, are truly the crux of the ROE debate.[25]

The just war criteria related to rules of engagement are those that acknowledge the necessity of using limited force to accomplish a defined mission, noncombatant immunity, and proportionality in the use of force. These criteria contain the broad framework; rules of engagement move from general ideas to specific application.

U.S. troops invaded Iraq on March 19, 2003, to remove Saddam Hussein from power, find and destroy weapons of mass destruction, and eliminate supporters of international terrorism. As it happened, Saddam Hussein was deposed, but no weapons of mass destruction were found, and Iraq's role in international terrorism came to be a debate topic, with reservations arising about Iraq's actual participation in sponsoring groups such as al-Qaeda. After Saddam's removal, the U.S. mission in Iraq evolved into an attempt to enshrine democracy in the Middle East, win allegiance of the Iraqi people to democratic ideals, and work with Iraqis to establish a cohesive government capable of leading a peaceful nation.

The U.S. military entered Iraq to depose Saddam Hussein, defeat forces loyal to Saddam and opposed to the United States, and establish conditions favorable for an independent democratic government. What happened after the defeat of Saddam and his military was that an insurgency, terrorism, and civil war erupted in Iraq. These are complicated phenomena, but, in essence, they can be explained as follows. The insurgency was comprised of Iraqi fighters who oppose the U.S. occupation of their country and who fight to harm or kill U.S. and other coalition forces so as to drive these forces out of Iraq. Terrorists, mostly from other Middle East countries, gained access to Iraq through poorly defended borders and struck at U.S. forces and contractors employed in the rebuilding of Iraq in order to undermine the occupation. Finally, in Iraq there are three distinct factions—the Kurds, the Shiites, and the Sunnis—and the Shiite and Sunni factions each want to be preeminent in government and use ambushes, kidnappings, bombings, and IEDs to accomplish this goal. U.S. forces act as peacekeepers who try to impose order; frequently they are targeted when they try to intervene to impose or maintain order. The mission of the U.S. military in Iraq has become the political task of assisting in the transition to forming a democratic Iraqi government. From the outset, many Iraqis did not want U.S. forces and, as we have seen, these forces face great danger from IEDs and car bombs. It goes without saying that if members of the U.S. armed forces kill civilians because they follow rules of engagement in dangerous situations, these agents of the U.S. government may undermine the essence of their mission because of the hostility they engender in the local population. While rational people would not hesitate to justify steps that soldiers take to protect themselves, it is clear that killing or injuring civilians or carrying out military maneuvers in Iraqi mosques are actions that inflame those very people that U.S. and coalition forces are trying to influence.

Rules of engagement instruct soldiers to protect themselves if they are in danger because they detect a hostile intention or anticipate a hostile action against them. On its face, this is reasonable, but, to the extent that military personnel are mistaken in perceiving a hostile intention or anticipating a hostile action, and they take defensive measures with deadly consequences, their actions yield dreadful results.

Good soldiers find themselves in a terribly compromised position. If they hold fire to give the foe the benefit of the doubt, they may lose their lives. If they do not hold fire, the persons they injure or kill may turn out to be innocent persons. This is a nightmare situation and, while the rules of engagement bring some clarity to the daily encounters of a soldier's life, they also yield results that are a dreadful burden both for individuals and for nations. With this in mind, it is of the utmost importance that leaders of a nation who consider the case for going to war be certain that there is a just cause, that the effort will likely be proportionate, and that they sincerely believe that there is no other way to resolve an apparent conflict.

Conclusion

Rules of engagement exist to instruct troops in means to use to defend themselves and in specific tactics to employ to accomplish their mission. Troops need to be able to react to hostile actions when they encounter them and to do so with sufficient force to defend themselves. Commanders are obligated to ensure that their subordinates are adequately instructed in how to take care of themselves. Commanders also need to advance the military mission that their nation has undertaken. Perhaps the most difficult task for those who formulate rules of engagement and those who carry them out is to exercise appropriate restraint so as to honor the just war tradition, which requires that the force that is used be proportionate to the perceived threat.

Questions for Discussion

1. Define *rules of engagement.*
2. What kinds of action by an enemy call for the use of lethal force?
3. Why are rules of engagement classified information?
4. From what kinds of persons and devices do U.S. military forces in Iraq face the gravest danger?
5. Describe one incident of civilian casualties following the use of force by U.S. troops and state why you approve or disapprove of the action taken by the troops.
6. Why were the U.S. pilots who fired in error on Canadian soldiers in Afghanistan in 2002 convicted of misconduct?

7. Comment on this statement from this chapter: "Troops on the ground will live with the consequences of their choices for the rest of their lives, and a burdened conscience is a terrible weight to carry."
8. Commanders need to safeguard the safety of troops on the ground and advance the military mission in which the nation is engaged. Discuss issues and conflicts that accompany this dual responsibility.

Case Study

Two soldiers are on duty at a checkpoint in a city south of Baghdad. A school bus approaches and fails to slow down. It is a very hot day, the windows on the school bus are open, and the soldiers can hear children's chatter. There are signs on the road in Arabic and English, telling drivers to slow down. Hand signals by the soldiers have been ignored. One of the soldiers has fired warning shots, and the other soldier, seated in an armored tank, is taking aim at the windshield of the bus.

1. Based on what you know about political and military strategy and the rules of engagement, what do you think these soldiers should do? Why?
2. Based on what you know of the just war criteria, what do you think these soldiers should do? Why?
3. If the soldiers do not fire on the bus, what explanation are they likely to offer?
4. If the soldiers do fire on the bus, what explanation are they likely to offer?

CHAPTER FOUR

FIGHTING THE WAR ON TERROR WHILE HONORING THE JUST WAR TRADITION

Terrorism is the face of war in the new millennium. Terrorists are groups of individuals who are united by an ideology or philosophy as well as by opposition to a religion, a way of life, a nation, an organization, a group, or some other collectivity. In order to advance their ideas or inflict harm on a group they differ with, terrorists resort to a wide range of harmful tactics. Strictly speaking, terrorists do not go *to war* because they do not represent nations and they do not possess the armaments or personnel assets contained in a nation's military capacity. Aspects of terrorism that make it particularly difficult to defend against are the secrecy about who adheres to its beliefs and the surprise nature of its attacks. Since, for the most part, the weapons terrorists use are procured from sources other than national defense stockpiles, terrorists improvise and use items like homemade explosives or civilian airplanes to carry out their attacks. (A few rogue nations violate international protocols by selling weapons to terrorist organizations. A case in point is Iran, which allegedly supplied the Lebanon-based terror organization Hezbollah with rockets that Hezbollah used to attack Israel in July 2006.)

It is frightening to imagine what other tactics terrorists might employ in the future, but detonating explosives hidden in commercial shipping containers or exploding dirty bombs containing nuclear materials are two especially troubling possibilities.

A definition of terrorism offered by the Central Intelligence Agency and contained in Title 22 of the U.S. Code, Section 2656f(d) reads as follows:

The term "terrorism" means premeditated, politically motivated violence perpetrated against noncombatant targets by subnational groups or clandestine agents, usually intended to influence an audience.

The term "international terrorism" means terrorism involving the territory or the citizens of more than one country.

The term "terrorist group" means any group that practices, or has significant subgroups that practice, international terrorism.[1]

Terrorist Attacts on U.S. Soil

Since 1993, the United States has been targeted by several terrorist attacks, including five that we review here.

The first attack we discuss, on the World Trade Center in New York City in 1993, took the United States by surprise and made people aware that there are groups of foreign terrorists who are intent on harming the nation.

On February 26, 1993 at 12:17 PM, a Ryder truck filled with 1,500 pounds of explosives was parked by terrorists and detonated in the underground garage of the north tower, opening a 30m hole through 4 sublevels of concrete. Six people were killed and over a thousand injured.

Six Islamist extremist conspirators were convicted of the crime in 1994 and 1998 and given prison sentences of 240 years each. According to a presiding judge, the conspirators' chief aim at the time of the attack was to destabilize the north tower and send it crashing into the south tower, toppling both landmarks.[2]

Two years later, on April 19, 1995, in an attack carried out by U.S. citizens, a horrific bombing took place in Oklahoma City.

Just after parents dropped their children off at the day care center at the Murrah Federal Building in downtown

Oklahoma City, a massive bomb inside a Ryder Rental Truck and supplemental charges inside the building, blew half of the nine-story building into oblivion, killing 168 people and injuring hundreds of others.[3]

The so-called war on terror was undertaken in response to third set of attacks we discuss, those of September 11, 2001, on the World Trade Center and the Pentagon. Nineteen men, members of al-Qaeda, hijacked four civilian airplanes and used three planes as missiles, flying them into the twin towers of the World Trade Center and into the Pentagon. Within a few hours of the attacks on the World Trade Center, the twin towers collapsed. Following an altercation between hijackers and passengers on board a fourth plane, United Airlines Flight 93 crashed in farmland in Pennsylvania and did not reach its target, which likely was a landmark building in Washington, D.C., such as the White House or the Capitol. More than three thousand people were killed in these attacks, along with the hijackers.

Beginning on September 18, 2001, one week after the attacks of 9/11, anthrax mailings started in the United States and continued over the course of several weeks. The last known victim, Ottile Lundgren, ninety-four, died on November 21, 2001.

Letters containing anthrax bacteria were mailed to news media offices and two U.S. Senators, killing five people, most of them postal workers who handled the mail. The crime remains unsolved. Twenty-two people developed anthrax infections, eleven of the life-threatening inhalation variety.[4]

The Beltway sniper attacks, the fifth set of terrorist attacks we consider, took place during three weeks of October 2002 in the Maryland–Virginia–Washington, D.C., area. Ten people were killed and three others critically injured by U.S. citizens who were spree killers and who shot people, selected at random, and then fled in their car. It was later learned that the rampage apparently had begun the month before, with murders and robbery in other states that had resulted in three deaths. These attacks terrorized people in this area, who tried to alter their normal routines so as not to be targets for the snipers.

The terrorist attacks just outlined were different in kind and were evaluated differently by police and government leaders.

World Trade Center (1993). After the 1993 explosion in the garage of the World Trade Center, the primary understanding of what had happened was that a strategically important financial center in the United States had been attacked by a group of ideological terrorists. The main emphases in the response were to locate those responsible and bring them to justice. FBI and police officials succeeded in doing this in a very short period of time. They traced the truck that was used to carry the explosives to a rental agency and laid a trap for those who rented the vehicle. Four of the five culprits who carried out the attack walked into the trap: Mohammad Salameh, Nidal Ayyad, Mahmud Abouhalima, and Ahmad Mohammad Ajaj. These men were convicted of federal charges on March 4, 1994, and they were each sentenced to 240 years in prison without the possibility of parole.[5] A fifth man who was involved in the bombing, Ramzi Ahmed Yousef, who escaped to Pakistan immediately after the attack, was captured there in February 1995. Yousef was returned to the United States where, on January 8, 1998, he was convicted and sentenced to 240 years in prison with the highly unusual recommendation from the judge that he be kept in solitary confinement for the rest of his life.[6] Sheikh Abdul Rahman was the final terrorist convicted in conjunction with the bombing, and he is serving a life sentence in federal prison. The first bombing at the World Trade Center triggered a limited response aimed at apprehending the terrorists who planned and carried it out, and meting out severe penalties to them.

Murrah Federal Building (1995). The second terrorist act reviewed involved the bombing of a federal office building and the largest loss of life on U.S. soil from a terrorist act up until 1995. Chillingly, included in the 168 victims were nineteen children from an on-site day care center. Again, police authorities and FBI agents approached this monstrous deed with the principal intent of identifying and capturing the criminals who bombed the building. As with the 1993 bombing in New York City, law enforcement authorities did their work quickly and efficiently. Just eighty minutes after the blast, in a routine traffic stop, an Oklahoma State Trooper picked up Timothy McVeigh because McVeigh was driving a car without license plates. McVeigh's arrest resulted in his detention, during which time officials identified him as the mastermind of the bombing of the federal building. Earplugs that he carried with him and other incriminating evidence on his person and in his car led police to consider him a possible suspect in the bombing; their suspicions were soon borne out, and McVeigh was charged. Within a few days, Terry Nichols, McVeigh's accomplice, was also apprehended. McVeigh and Nichols were brought to trial in federal court in Denver, and McVeigh was sentenced to death. He was executed on June 11, 2001. On August 9, 2004, Terry Nichols received 161 life sentences, one for each of the people who died in the bombing. Two acquaintances of McVeigh and Nichols who knew about the planned bombing, a husband and wife named Michael and Lori Fortier, were also apprehended in conjunction with this case. Michael Fortier helped McVeigh survey the Murrah building and he assisted with assembling the explosives. In order to procure immunity from prosecution for his wife, Fortier cooperated with the prosecution and testified against McVeigh and Nichols. In exchange for his cooperation, Fortier received a twelve-year prison sentence, and his wife escaped prosecution. Fortier was released from prison on January 20, 2005, after serving ten and one-half years of his sentence.[7]

Beltway Snipers (2002). Intense publicity from the media, exhaustive detective work by police and FBI, contact with a telephone hotline by one of the snipers, and identification and eventual publication of the license plate number of the sniper's car were the factors that resulted in apprehension of two men who carried out the Beltway attacks.

> The sniper attacks ended on October 24, 2002 when police arrested John Allen Muhammad and Lee Boyd Malvo at a highway rest area in Maryland after receiving two telephone tips from alert citizens. It was later

learned that the three-week-long rampage was motivated, at least in part, by a plot to extort $10 million
from government agencies.[8]

John Allen Muhammad was convicted in Virginia of four charges,
including capital murder, and, on March 9, 2004, he was sentenced to death.[9] Lee Boyd Malvo was convicted of murder and
sentenced on March 10, 2004, to life in prison without the possibility of parole.[10]

Thus, with the first attack on the World Trade Center, the
bombing of the Murrah Federal Building in Oklahoma, and the
Beltway sniper attacks, apprehension of suspects occurred as a
result of collaboration between police and FBI and courts in the
United States meted out punishment to the terrorists.

For now, we will bracket the attacks of 9/11 and return to
them after we consider how the United States responded to the
anthrax attacks.

Anthrax (2001). One week after the attacks of September 11, 2001,
the anthrax mailings began. As of this writing, no one has been
charged with the crime, more than two dozen people have been
sickened, and at least five have died. Two of those who died were
postal workers who handled anthrax-laced letters as part of their
jobs, and a third was a photo editor from America Media, Inc., in
Florida. Two women were also infected and died. Authorities have
not been able to determine how these women came into contact
with anthrax.

As word of sickness and death spread throughout the United
States, people became anxious about the threat of anthrax. A few
men have been identified by the media as suspects, but no one has
been charged. The emphases of law enforcement officials are on
apprehension of the terrorist mailer and subsequent trial and
punishment by the judiciary so as to safeguard the public from
this person. To this end, the FBI has developed a profile of the
anthrax mailer—a description of the type of person likely to carry
out these attacks—derived from psychological and scientific
probabilities. This profile should not be approached as a precise

description, but, rather, it is to be used as a general guideline in the task of tracking down the guilty party. The bureau is guided by this analysis as it tries to apprehend the anthrax terrorist.

The main aspects of the profile are that the anthrax mailer is likely a man who works alone and has access to laboratory equipment such as a microscope, glassware, and centrifuge. He has access to anthrax and probably has ways to ensure his own safety while working with this highly dangerous substance. This person has knowledge of the Trenton, New Jersey, area because he used mailboxes and post offices in this vicinity. The mailer did not target his victims randomly, having deliberately sent letters to NBC News, the *New York Post*, the office of Sen. Tom Daschle, and the offices of American Media, Inc. Perhaps he held grudges for years, vowing to get even with his targets. The motive for these grudges is unknown.[11]

RESPONDING TO 9/11

Let us now return to the most dreadful terrorist attacks in U.S. history: the events of September 11, 2001, in which civilian planes were commandeered and used as bombs to carry out the destruction of highly important buildings in New York City and Washington, D.C., and result in the deaths of approximately three thousand people. As the attacks were being carried out, President George W. Bush was in Sarasota, Florida, for a scheduled appearance at an elementary school. Bush had been president for less than nine months, and in those nine months the subjects of terrorism and terrorist attacks against the United States had not been part of his public agenda; these topics were also far from the minds of Americans.

In the aftermath of the attacks, President Bush was swiftly moved by airplane to a secure location, and he and his advisors, shocked and sickened by the attacks, tried to comprehend and respond to what happened. When his assistant Andrew Card told the president that a second plane had hit the World Trade Center, the president's reaction was, "They had declared war on us, and I made up my mind at that moment that we were going to war."[12] This is a key development in that President Bush, from the very first moments after the attacks of 9/11, decided to fight a war against the forces that had "declared war" on the United States by engaging in terrorist actions against the nation. The military forces of the nation would carry out this war; unlike responses to the other four terrorist incidents described, apprehension by police, assisted by investigative agencies, would not be the way to justice. Rather, there would be a war against terrorists and terrorism in which investigative agencies would play a part, but the larger contribution would be made by military forces. Early in the war, on February 1, 2002, in the State of the Union address, President Bush said:

> When I called our troops into action, I did so with complete confidence in their courage and skill. And tonight, thanks to them, we are winning the war on terror. The men and women of our Armed Forces have delivered a message now clear to every enemy of the United States: Even 7,000 miles away, across oceans and continents, on mountaintops and in caves—you will not escape the justice of this nation.[13]

President Bush's first front in the war against terror was Afghanistan, where al-Qaeda fighters, the followers of Osama bin Laden, trained in remote camps in the mountainous nation and where U.S. intelligence officials believed bin Laden was hiding. Tribal leaders, known as the Taliban, who supported or tolerated bin Laden and al-Qaeda, were killed or removed from positions of power, terrorists were killed or captured and imprisoned, and a new government, democratically elected and allied to the United States, was established.

At the same time that military operations were proceeding in Afghanistan, U.S. intelligence agencies were operating to uncover and disrupt the financial and communications infrastructure of the terrorist group known as al-Qaeda. Although it is impossible to calculate the level of success of U.S. operations against al-Qaeda, there is general agreement that the operations of this group have been severely disrupted by the actions taken against it.

Fighting the War on Terror

On March 19, 2003, President Bush continued and extended the war against the terrorists who attacked the United States by ordering U.S. forces to invade Iraq and render that nation incapable of providing state support for terrorism. In the run-up to war,

> the administration took a forceful stand against Iraq over its alleged possession of weapons of mass destruction and its resistance to UN arms inspections. Congress authorized the use of the military against Iraq, and the United States continued to build up its forces in the Middle East. Although in November (2002) the Security Council passed a resolution offering Iraq a "final opportunity" to cooperate on arms inspections, which subsequently resumed, it became clear that Bush was determined on a course of "pre-emptive war" to prevent Iraq from developing or possessing weapons of mass destruction that might someday be used against the United States. This use of pre-emptive war to protect the United States, often called the "Bush doctrine," was adopted by the administration in its National Security Strategy (2002). A significant shift in official U.S. policy, it was the result, in part, of the September 11th attacks.[14]

Iraqi President Saddam Hussein was considered an enemy of the United States and a supporter of terrorism, and his removal from office was one of the major goals of the U.S. military engagement in Iraq. As his government collapsed on April 9, 2003, Hussein fled from his presidential palace in Baghdad and U.S. and coalition forces took control of the city. Eight months later, on December 14, 2003, Saddam Hussein was captured near his birthplace in Tikrit and arrested as a war criminal based on his alleged role in mass executions of Iraqi Shiites who resisted his dictatorship. Hussein was tried in Baghdad for war crimes and, on November 5, 2006, was convicted and sentenced to death by hanging. He was executed on December 30, 2006.

Ethical Questions Faced by Military Personnel Engaged in Fighting the War on Terror

Since 2001, the United States has deployed as many as one million troops to Iraq and Afghanistan.[15] As we have seen, following the attacks on September 11, 2001, President George W. Bush decided that the United States would go to war against the terrorist network that attacked this country. In responding to the 1993 attack against the World Trade Center, the Oklahoma City bombing, and the Beltway sniper attacks, police and FBI agents located and arrested those who were responsible, and the U.S. justice system handed down appropriate sentences. Military forces were not involved in apprehension or retribution. President Bush decided that September 11 was a manifestation of a much larger threat and called for a different kind of response. He exercised the prerogatives of the commander-in-chief of the nation's military forces in embarking on a war against terrorism.

It is up to each and every one of the individuals in uniform to carry out the president's political and military policy, and these men and women find themselves facing difficult ethical questions as they do so. Waging a war on terror entails perplexing questions, many of which are being faced by members of the armed forces for the first time. Let us examine these questions as we attempt to understand in what a morally appropriate response would consist.

MEETING CRITERIA FOR JUST CAUSE AND LAST RESORT

If civilian leaders do not make a convincing case that there is a just cause for going to war and that war is a last resort, are members of the military required to take up arms to fight in an elective, preemptive war? President George W. Bush said that the war that the United States and its coalition partners began on March 19, 2003, was undertaken at a time of our choosing and justified resort to arms by saying, "The United States of America has the sovereign authority to use force in assuring its own national security."[16] Individual members of the armed forces who are on the ground fighting wars do not have access to the classified information on which presidents base their decisions and calculations. Nevertheless, these men and women do the tasks of war, the worst of which require that they kill the enemy and be at risk of death and injury themselves. This is their professional duty, the true cost of military service. Not only are their lives at stake, their honor, too, is on the line as they decide whether or not to put themselves in harm's way and whom they will target in the course of doing their jobs. The justification for their actions depends on whether they are really fighting to assure the national security of their country, the cause for which the president declared war. Additionally, the issue of whether all reasonable paths to a peaceful resolution of disputes were exhausted before the nation's leadership committed the armed forces to war is a critically important element in justifying participation in an elective war.

Did the United States undertake military action in Iraq to prevent terrorists supplied by Iraq from harming the homeland at some time in the future? Or did President Bush order the invasion in order to preempt an attack by Iraq, or terrorists supplied by Iraq, that was certain and soon to come? Preemption of an attack is accepted by just war thinkers as a reasonable premise for going to war, while preventing a vague future attack that is far from certain is not considered a just cause. And the burden of proof lies with the nation that first engages in belligerent action. In this regard, contemporary just war theorist Michael Walzer writes:

> A real preemptive war begins with a decision to attack an enemy that we know is about to attack us. The attack is literally on its way; we see it coming. We move to strike first so as to avoid the dangers of waiting to be hit. The classic example is Israel in 1967.
>
> Preventive war aims to ward off a much more distant threat, a speculative threat, that may or may not materialize somewhere down the road, and which might be dealt with through deterrence or alliance or diplomacy. There are other things to do.

· ·

Now, it is possible to make an argument that the line between preemption and prevention is harder to draw today, in an age of rapid delivery systems and weapons of mass destruction. But the containment regime imposed on Iraq after the first Gulf War was—or we can now think of it as—an experiment in addressing this new kind of threat: using force, but short of war. And we had good reasons in 2002 and 2003 to think that the experiment was working, at least with regard to weapons of mass destruction and long-range delivery systems. It is not so successful, as we are now learning, with regard to conventional weapons. But it was successful enough to make full-scale war unnecessary— and, if unnecessary, then unjust.[17]

The invasion of Iraq met with more approval at the outset than it has as time has passed. In March 2003, the Bush administration made the case that Saddam Hussein was abetting terrorism and engaged in procuring weapons of mass destruction that might be used against the United States. The war against Iraq was undertaken to depose Hussein and to destroy Iraqi stockpiles of weapons of mass destruction as well as Iraqi capacity to produce these weapons in the future. The case was made that the war was preemptive, not preventive.

As it turned out, Saddam Hussein was quickly driven from office and subsequently captured. His alleged support for terrorism and alliances with terrorists were not substantiated. No weapons of mass destruction or facilities for manufacture of such weapons were found.

Congressman John Murtha (D, PA), a decorated Vietnam veteran and longtime member of Congress, said that if he were eligible, he would not join the military today. By way of explanation, Murtha said:

The military had no problem recruiting directly after 9/11 because everyone understood that we had been attacked. But now the military's ability to attract

recruits is being hampered by the prospect of pro-
longed, extended and repeated deployments; inade-
quate equipment; shortened home stays; the lack of
any connection between Iraq and the brutal attacks of
9/11; and—most importantly—the administration's
constantly changing, undefined, open-ended military
mission in Iraq.[18]

While Murtha's comments are hypothetical, relating to what
he would do if he were a young man in today's world, the comments are relevant to the situations of men and women who are
serving in the military now as well as those who are considering
the possibility of enlisting. The reason that they are relevant is
that an individual needs to be convinced of the moral rightness
and military necessity of the cause his or her nation pursues. If
individuals cannot concur that a military engagement is defensible on moral or strategic grounds, they should not enlist. And, if
they believe the decision to go to war was not a last resort, they
will have trouble embracing an undertaking that could have been
accomplished by less deadly means. If they are on active duty, the
situation becomes more complicated, but, if one were to follow
the same argument through to its logical conclusion, it would
result in the suggestion that even active duty forces who consider
the reasons for their mission questionable should think about
asking to be relieved of their duties.

MEETING THE CRITERION FOR PROPORTIONALITY

It is up to civilian leaders to decide on the issue of proportionality—that is, whether more good will be achieved from military action than the harm it will inevitably cause—but what is a
soldier to do who does not concur in the calculation of the leadership? This question becomes germane as a war progresses. At
the outset of hostilities, the soldier and the citizen have little
choice other than to trust the commander-in-chief. It is the president who has access to a comprehensive account of the nation's
military capabilities as well as how this measures up against the
potential of the opposition. The president and the president's

advisors are also in a position to estimate, based on probabilities, the risks and costs of war against the likelihood of achieving the goals that the nation seeks through combat. If, as a war progresses, members of the armed forces, who have firsthand knowledge of military engagements and their consequences, begin to realize that whatever good is being achieved is vastly disproportionate to the harm that is being done, and see little or no progress toward attaining stated goals, it would be incumbent upon individuals to face this fact and consider their options. Governments do not make arrangements for members of the armed forces to withdraw based on their appraisals of how things are going. This fact underscores the reality that the choice faced by individuals in the armed forces is an ethically unacceptable one: to continue to fight a war that, in their opinions, cannot be justified because the harm wrought is disproportionate to the good possibly to be attained, or to cease fighting in order to preserve personal integrity, thus risking severe penalties for abandoning their posts.

DECIDING TO WAGE WAR ON TERRORISTS INSTEAD OF COUNTERING TERRORISM BY OTHER MEANS

Will armed conflict against terrorists be more effective than other tactics against terrorist leaders, terrorist cells, and insurgent movements? Armed conflict in a war requires that large numbers of troops be sent to carry out the policies of civilian leaders. These troops receive training when they join the military or the reserves, and they receive additional training before deployment. In spite of this training, however, members of the armed forces who are sent to fight an unconventional war in urban areas are placed in a compromised position. In a sense, U.S. and coalition forces in Iraq are in uncharted waters, and they are part of a war characterized by unseen, constant dangers. Improvised explosive devices (IEDs) and car bombs have brought thousands of deaths to coalition forces and Iraqi civilians. In contrast, traditional fire fights with enemy forces have not occurred with much frequency. Tragically, in Iraq a vastly disproportionate number of civilians have died in the course of roadside, suicide, and car bombings.

Fighting the War on Terror

When President George W. Bush announced the U.S. intention to carry out military actions in Iraq, he assured the Iraqi people that the United States was not the enemy of Iraqi civilians.

> Many Iraqis can hear me tonight in a translated radio broadcast. And I have a message for them. If we must begin a military campaign, it will be directed against the lawless men who rule your country and not against you. As our coalition takes away their power we will deliver the food and medicine you need. We will tear down the apparatus of terror. And we will help you to build a new Iraq that is prosperous and free.[19]

Almost five years into the war in Iraq, civilians deal with violence in the streets, hostilities between rival Sunni and Shiite factions, foreign fighters, shortages of necessities, lack of electricity, unemployment, and delays in bringing oil production to anticipated levels. Training Iraqis to become members of the armed forces or police is especially frustrating because of frequent attacks on police and military training centers.

In terms of civilian casualties, in January 2006 President Bush said, "30,000 Iraqis, more or less, have died as a result of the initial incursion and the ongoing violence against Iraqis."[20] Iraqi civilians, who at the outset were assured that the war had nothing to do with them, suffer unimaginable harm and death as a result of warfare in their midst. On the positive side, the Iraqi people are rid of Saddam Hussein, a despotic ruler, and started on the road to democracy, with a provisional constitution in place as of June 30, 2004, and elections held to form a representative government in December 2005. Disputes among political and religious factions in Iraq following the 2005 elections were finally resolved on May 20, 2006, when the Iraqi parliament approved a unity government whose members were appointed for a term of four years. The new prime minister, Nouri al-Maliki, filled key positions on June 8, 2006.

> The selection of an interior minister, a defense minister and a national security adviser gives Iraq a complete

government for the first time since elections in December 2005 and it provides a key opportunity to promote political reconciliation between members of the country's Sunni Muslim minority and the Shiite-dominated government.[21]

The major issue facing the new government is the need to suppress violence throughout the country and secure the nation so that it can provide civil order for the Iraqi people. The Iraq Project of the Brookings Institution estimates the number of Iraqi military killed during the first three years of the war at more than sixty thousand.[22] The U.S. military has not kept body counts since the Vietnam War; hence, there are no official numbers of enemy deaths recorded by the U.S. government.

Members of the U.S. armed forces cannot avoid asking themselves the question, "In view of the numbers of dead and wounded and the chaos caused by war, was the downside of the war worth the advantages gained by the Iraqis, or should non-military initiatives been taken to deal with the perceived terrorist threats coming from Iraq?" For example, in the months prior to the coalition invasion, United Nations arms inspectors had been on the ground in Iraq, looking for banned weapons and unable to locate them. The arms inspectors were willing to continue to look for the weapons, but they left following the decision by President Bush to invade the country. Furthermore, many allies of the United States, including Canada, Germany, and France, did not join the coalition because they did not concur in the need to invade Iraq at that time. It is too late to undo what has occurred, but it is important that this issue be debated so that civilian leaders learn important lessons for the future. It is important, too, for troops on the ground who need to be convinced of the rightness of waging war so as to be of good conscience.

THE STATUS OF TERRORISTS

If a nation goes to war against terrorism, are the terrorists who are targeted equivalent to enemy combat forces? There are two ways to answer this question. The first is that, since terrorists are not part of an organized armed force subject to a national leader, they are different from what have traditionally been understood as enemy combat forces and, therefore, are not entitled to be treated according to the standards of the just war tradition. According to this way of thinking, terrorists are illegal combatants and troops who oppose them do not owe terrorists humane considerations required by the just war tradition.

The second way to answer the question is that terrorists do not wage war wearing uniforms, as subjects to a national leader, or by so-called conventional means. Nevertheless, if their goal is to fight a nation or nations, then, as fighters against a nation, they are more akin to enemy combat forces than to any other classifiable group. Given the purview of this book, the significance of this question is that it leads to deciding whether or not the rules of war, as these have been formulated over two millennia, apply to combat against terrorists. If the rules of war apply, members of the armed forces would need to practice restraint based on the moral limits inherent in the just war tradition. If the rules of war do not apply, then what legal basis would there be for members of the armed forces to reject barbaric tactics in fighting terrorists?

In 2001, John C. Yoo was a deputy assistant attorney general in John Ashcroft's office; Ashcroft was attorney general of the United States. Because his area of expertise was foreign affairs and war powers issues, Yoo had a large role in addressing the status of foreign terrorists. He drafted influential opinions, many of which remain classified, "including one that said the Geneva Conventions did not apply" when captives were suspected terrorists, and "at least two others that countenanced the use of highly coercive interrogation techniques on suspected terrorists."[23]

The question, "Are captured terrorists entitled to be treated according to international treaties such as the Geneva Conventions?" is directly related to whether or not terrorists are similar enough to enemy combatants to be placed in the same category. The Geneva Conventions give detailed instructions about how humane treatment of prisoners of war is to be carried out as well as the right of persons accused of crime to a fair trial. All nations agree to meet these standards, thus ensuring that captives, whether they are healthy or wounded, are treated with respect, allowed visits from the Red Cross, and adequately provided for.

If terrorists are not entitled to the basic humane treatment prescribed by the Geneva Conventions, does this mean that they should be denied fundamental human rights as traditionally understood? It was terrorists without conscience who carried out the attacks of September 11, 2001, which resulted in the deaths of approximately three thousand people, most of whom were civilians. Should U.S. and coalition forces who capture alleged terrorists practice restraint and humane consideration as they incarcerate, interrogate, and detain individuals from al-Qaeda?

This question is an unsettling one, and it raises fundamental questions about the kind of war in which the United States is engaged. On the one hand, passions are aroused and people tend to reason that our forces should not have their hands tied behind their backs as they try to apprehend terrorists and prevent future incidents of terrorism. On the other hand, fundamental insights of the just war tradition should not be overlooked or rationalized away. Implicit in the Geneva Conventions are several reasons to respect prisoners. In regard to reciprocity, it is assumed that if one side treats prisoners properly, the other side will follow suit. In regard to right intention, it is understood that full justice probably does not exist on one side while no justice exists on the other. Therefore, captors ought to allow for the possibility that the captive is fighting for a cause he believes to be just and is following a person he considers to be an upright leader. It is also possible that an individual captive has been captured in error and harbors no hostility toward the United States or its coalition partners. In regard to captives who are enemies, captors need to resist an inclination to be swayed by propaganda that suggests that the enemy is less than human and not entitled to respect or consideration. If captors look at a captive in this way and act based on such an insight, this would result in acts of barbarism that undermine the integrity of captors and the justification of the cause to which they are committed.

Seeking to defend the Bush administration against charges that it tolerates policies that result in improper treatment of detainees, U.S. Secretary of State Condoleeza Rice said in

December 2005, "As a matter of U.S. policy, the United States' obligations under the CAT [United Nations Convention Against Torture], which prohibits, of course, cruel and inhumane and degrading treatment, those obligations extend to U.S. personnel wherever they are."[24]

The reasoning of the U.S. Supreme Court, in its June 29, 2006, ruling in *Hamdan v. Rumsfeld*, rejected the rationale of John C. Yoo that captured terrorists fall into a different category from enemy war combatants and are not entitled to trials in accordance with U.S. standards of justice or the standards contained in the U.S. Uniform Code of Military Justice. The majority on the court (five members) ruled that the Constitution does not give the president and the executive branch authority to act without congressional authorization to set up special trials before military commissions for suspected terrorists because military commissions deny legal safeguards to suspects. Specifically, the rights to examine evidence against them and the ability to appeal convictions to judicial rather than executive branch entities would not be safeguarded by military commissions. Additionally, the Supreme Court ruled that Common Article 3 of the Geneva Conventions applies to imprisoned terrorist suspects and that they are entitled to the protections asserted in this article, which was quoted in its entirety in chapter 1 of this book.

John C. Yoo expressed disagreement with the Supreme Court's decision, contending that the court's reasoning in *Hamdan* may signal the collapse of the entire enterprise put in place to deal decisively with terrorists, which accorded a great deal of discretion to the executive branch. "It could affect detention conditions, interrogation methods, the use of force," he said. "It could affect every aspect of the war on terror."[25] Yoo is correct in his assessment of the Supreme Court ruling, because this ruling establishes that even if terrorists are classified as illegal combatants, this does not negate the responsibility of the U.S. president and armed forces to act in accordance with the just war tradition.

The Supreme Court's decision in *Hamdan v. Rumsfeld* prompted the Bush administration to ask congressional leaders to enact legislation establishing military commissions and delineating the specific rights of detainees who would be tried by these commissions. Congress passed the Military Commissions Act in September 2006, and President Bush signed the act on October 17, 2006. Supporters of the new law contend that illegal combatants present a grave threat to the United States and that they will be treated fairly when tried by these commissions. They will not receive the same legal rights as U.S. citizens, or even those afforded to legal enemy combatants, because they are not entitled to these rights; however, they will get fair trials.

Critics of the legislation maintain that detainees will have no means of contesting their detention until after they are tried and convicted, which could be years or decades after their arrest. Further, U.S. citizens who might be arrested and detained because they are suspected of posing threats as illegal enemy combatants would be stripped of the rights of citizens after being detained. Finally, those who object to the new legislation argue that it gives the president too much discretion regarding interrogation techniques and how the stipulations of the Geneva Conventions are to be interpreted. To date, there have been no trials of illegal enemy combatants by military commissions, and many commentators anticipate court challenges about the legality of these commissions.

RESPONDING TO THE INSURGENCY

The U.S. invasion of Iraq precipitated an insurgency, with the result that Iraqis are fighting against coalition forces as well as against opposing factions in their own nation, such as Sunni Arabs against Shiite Arabs, and both these religious groups against criminal gangs. Insurgents want coalition forces to leave their country, and they want the religious or secular faction to which they belong to hold the most power in the government. The most radical of the insurgents are known as *Muhajadeen,* or holy warriors, and they want the Iraqi government to impose *Sharia,* or religious rule according to the Koran.[26]

This situation puts U.S. and coalition forces in a very difficult ethical position as they try to defend themselves against people who, at the outset, were not their opponents and whose major issue with the coalition is that it is an occupying force.

What issues does this fact raise for individual members of the military? If, at the outset, there was a reason to fight terrorists, as the war progressed U.S. and coalition forces found themselves fighting Iraqis who want the U.S. and coalition forces to leave, the question becomes, "What are U.S. troops supposed to do?" Some of those the United States led coalition fights against are terrorists, most of whom entered Iraq from porous borders with other nations in the Middle East, but the vast majority are Iraqis who want to oust the occupiers. If members of the military argue that they will not continue with a problematic mission that is causing turmoil for Iraqis and grave danger for them, their position would be reasonable. On the other hand, if members of the military accept the position of the Bush administration and remain on active duty in order to provide security for the Iraqi people and prevent the country from disintegrating into chaos, their professionalism should be respected. Raising this question underscores the disconnect between the stated reason for the invasion and the changing circumstances since April 2003, when Saddam Hussein was deposed.

NONCOMBATANT IMMUNITY

When fighting takes place in a populated area, how can civilians be kept from harm? When unmanned drone aircraft are used to bomb suspected terrorist locations, what precautions should be taken to avoid harm to civilians? When coalition forces are carrying out operations in populated areas, civilians can be warned to leave or to stay out of harm's way when there is fighting in the streets. Such directions will lessen harm to civilians but will not eliminate death and injury. Many of the deaths to civilians in Iraq have come at the hands of insurgents who make political statements by targeting coalition forces or Iraqi police forces, or political or religious leaders, with suicide bombs, IEDs, or car bombs. Detonations are not announced in advance, and the death toll to civilians since the breakdown of civil order in Iraq has been staggering. Controlling what insurgents do when they act with disregard for the rights of civilians is not the responsibility of coalition forces. This issue brings us back to the proportionality stipulation of the just war criteria. The president needed to calculate that the good to be achieved by the war effort would outweigh the evils that are an inevitable consequence of war. As the war has progressed, the tide of public opinion has turned against the decision to go to war, and a consensus among the majority of people in the United States is that the war in Iraq was a mistake. According to a *Washington Post*–ABC News Poll in June 2005, more than two years after the start of the war,

> nearly three-quarters of Americans say the number of casualties in Iraq is unacceptable, while two-thirds say the U.S. military there is bogged down and nearly six in 10 say the war was not worth fighting—in all three cases matching or exceeding the highest levels of pessimism yet recorded. More than four in 10 believe the U.S. presence in Iraq is becoming analogous to the experience in Vietnam.[27]

A Zogby poll released on January 15, 2006, showed even less support for President Bush's handling of the Iraq War. "Just 34% of respondents said Mr. Bush was doing a good or excellent job managing the war, down from 38% approval in a Zogby poll taken in mid-October 2005."[28]

For troops on the ground, the issue of whether or not, in view of death and harm to civilians, they can continue to be part of the Iraqi war is a constant issue. As far as civilian deaths from attacks by drone airplanes are concerned, the purpose of these attacks is to kill terrorist leaders when intelligence reports that they are in specific locations. Intelligence agencies provide the location and then the details of targeting are worked out at command headquarters. These attacks frequently involve both civilian deaths and deaths to suspected terrorists. On January 13, 2006, a missile strike in the village of Damadola, Pakistan, was apparently intended for, but missed, al-Qaeda's second-in-command, Ayman al-Zawahiri. However, Pakistani officials say it killed at least three other top al-Qaeda members, including a chemical weapons expert.[29] In addition to the al-Qaeda deaths, an estimated eighteen civilians, including women and children, were killed. This attack prompted protests and anti–U.S. rhetoric, such as the following:

> Banners and placards read: "American bombing on Pakistan is the result of policies of [Pakistan] President Pervez Musharraf" and "Terrorist American troops should be expelled from Kashmir and Afghanistan." In the southern port of Karachi, the country's largest city, around 5,000 protestors took to the streets, chanting, "Do not kill innocent civilians in tribal areas" and "Anyone who is a friend of America is a traitor."[30]

While unmanned drone attacks are carried out by the CIA and not by members of the armed forces, the principle of noncombatant immunity still holds. The United States, in compliance with the just war tradition, can allow for some collateral deaths, but people all over the world questioned whether it was morally justified to kill eighteen innocent people in order to eliminate three terrorists. One could say that it depends on which side you take. A more satisfying answer is that civilians should not be thought of as expendable by a nation that values human dignity and human rights and that nation, the United States, should reject future attacks like the one at Damadola, Pakistan.

TREATMENT OF CAPTURED TERRORIST SUSPECTS

Several issues are raised about captured suspected terrorists: rendition, conditions of imprisonment, use of various techniques of interrogation, including torture, and cultural and religious sensitivity.

Rendition entails taking suspected terrorists to nations that allow very aggressive interrogation techniques for questioning in order to extract as much information about future terror plots as possible. Jane Mayer writes that rendition programs bear little relation to the system of due process afforded suspects of crimes in the United States. Terrorism suspects in Europe, Africa, Asia, and the Middle East have often been abducted by hooded or masked U.S. agents and then forced onto a Gulfstream V jet that has been registered to a series of dummy corporations. The jet has clearance to land at U.S. military bases. Upon arriving in foreign countries, rendered suspects often vanish. Detainees are not provided with lawyers, and often families are not informed of their whereabouts.[31]

The United States is founded on principles of justice that proclaim that a person is entitled to be charged with a crime and to have a fair trial. The Bush administration, arguing for rendition in cases where subjects are thought to be terrorists, said that terrorists do not have the same rights as U.S. citizens and that national security demands techniques such as rendition. Rendition, and what follows it, is obviously at variance with the spirit of the Geneva Conventions, which require that the human dignity of captives be respected and that prisoners not be brought to undisclosed locations and denied legal counsel or means to communicate with the outside world. Determining whether or not rendition is morally acceptable in the war on terror requires that one decide whether standards that mandate respect for human dignity as embodied in the Geneva Conventions are absolute or whether these standards can be circumvented under extreme circumstances. While the answer to the question will undoubtedly spark controversy, its importance and relevance are self-evident. Moreover, the issue of rendition is not one faced by typical troops on the ground but, rather, by operatives of intelligence services as well as those who order the capture and detention of suspected terrorists.

In the early days of the war on terror, the United States and its allies identified and apprehended many suspected terrorists in Afghanistan, and, as the war has continued, the United States located suspected terrorists in other countries such as Iraq and Pakistan. During the war in Iraq the classification given to suspected terrorist leaders was "high value targets." One of the first issues faced as suspected terrorists were captured was where to imprison them and, once a place or places had been determined, how to oversee their captivity. The United States decided to imprison terrorist suspects at Guantánamo Bay, Cuba, on part of the land the nation controls as a military installation. According to a Department of Defense news release, on July 20, 2005, there were approximately 510 detainees at Guantánamo.[32]

The issues with detention of suspected terrorists at Guantánamo and other sites, such as a prison facility near the airport in Baghdad, are that people are being held without charges, that dates for trials have not been set, and that they have been denied access to outside visitors, such as members of the International Red Cross. The Red Cross disagreed with the notion that detainees at Guantánamo fall into a separate category from other kinds of prisoners and make fewer claims on those who imprison them:

> The International Committee of the Red Cross has stated that, "Every person in enemy hands must have some status under international law: he is either a prisoner of war and, as such, covered by the Third Convention, a civilian covered by the Fourth Convention, [or] a member of the medical personnel of the armed forces who is covered by the First Convention. There is no intermediate status; nobody in enemy hands can fall outside the law." Thus, if the detainees are not classified as prisoners of war, this would still grant them the rights of the Fourth Geneva Convention (GCIV), as opposed to the more common Third Geneva Convention (GCIII) which deals exclusively with prisoners of war.[33]

At the outset of the war on terror, apprehending terror suspects and thwarting plots were the main goals of Bush administration policy, and these goals made sense. As suspects were captured, however, and removed from society, the treatment of imprisoned suspects became a significant question, because these people are entitled to defend themselves. If they are not terrorists, if they had no part in past or future plots against the United States or other nations, why should they be jailed? And, if they had part in a plot, there are degrees of complicity and punishment should fit the crime. The U.S. government, which stands for human rights and international standards of justice, needs to adhere to principles of justice in the detention centers it operates.

HOW JUST IS THE WAR ON TERROR?

Common Article 3, quoted in chapter 1 of this book, was recognized by the U.S. Supreme Court as applicable in regard to the prosecution of captives taken in the war on terror. As we have just seen, the United States came under criticism for conditions at the Guantánamo Bay, Cuba, detention facility because it was alleged that captured detainees who were suspected of working for al-Qaeda were not treated humanely as required by Article 3. Some human rights organizations, leaders of foreign governments, and U.S. citizens leveled these charges and then authorities took steps to prevent inhumane acts from occurring.

Additionally, on June 30, 2006, the U.S. Supreme Court in *Hamdan v. Rumsfeld* specified necessary conditions for conducting trials of detainees, relying primarily on the requirements of Common Article 3, section (d) that "all judicial guarantees which are recognized as indispensable by civilized peoples" needed to be met in adjudicating claims against suspected terrorists. (In so doing, the U.S. Supreme Court rejected the position of the Bush administration that allowed for trials by military commissions that would not include legal protections generally accorded to defendants in either military or civilian courts.)

One of the most disturbing issues that has come to light in conjunction with the war on terror is the way interrogation of detainees is carried out. The goal of interrogating a prisoner is to gain information so as to prevent future attacks. Innocent civilians are killed by terrorists and large areas can be destroyed. Economic and psychological impacts are terrible. If nuclear, biological, or chemical weapons are used in the future against a civilian target, the consequences will be horrific. With this in view, the importance of finding out what plans are in the making is apparent and the need to procure this information is self-evident. This fact brings us to the matter of torture and the questions of what techniques constitute torture and if torture is ever allowed. Writing in *Newsweek*, Evan Thomas and Michael Hirsh said:

A reconstruction of the road to *Abu Ghraib* shows why [the United States is being criticized for allowing torture techniques]: at each step, the Bush administration made understandable decisions to permit the use of harsh interrogation techniques against a few individuals. But the decisions were made in such an atmosphere of secrecy and confusion that the whole process spun out of control and produced atrocities that America may never live down.[34]

In an attempt to restore integrity to the U.S. management of detainees and its conduct of the war on terror, Congress passed and the president signed an amendment sponsored by Senators John McCain (R, AZ) and John Warner (R, VA) that was appended to a defense authorization bill and requires Defense Department personnel to observe the strictures in the *Army Field Manual for Intelligence Interrogation*. As for the CIA and other non–Defense Department personnel, the amendment would prohibit "cruel, inhuman, or degrading" treatment of detainees "regardless of nationality or physical location."[35] A revised edition of the *Army Field Manual*, containing detailed guidelines about interrogation techniques and specifically forbidding many actions that could be termed "torture," was released on September 6, 2006.

President Bush, in his December 30, 2005, signing statement with comments on the new law, seems to maintain that there might be circumstances under which he could direct that the law be side-stepped. "The executive branch shall construe [the law] in a manner consistent with the constitutional authority of the President... as Commander-in-Chief," Bush wrote, adding that this approach "will assist in achieving the shared objective of the Congress and the President...of protecting the American people from further terrorist attacks."[36] By so stating, the president is essentially hedging on the moral force of an absolute ban on torture. However, the spotlight on American treatment of detainees, together with the debate during which the immoral features of torture were elaborated, have combined to make it unlikely that acts of torture will happen in U.S.-run facilities.

Michael Ignatieff lays out rationale supportive of resorting to torture in extreme cases as well as reasons for an absolute ban against torture, which he favors.[37] As far as the exceptional case is concerned, "one where lives can be saved by the application of physical methods that amount to torture" is concerned, Ignatieff acknowledges that many U.S. citizens would not oppose torture in such circumstances. But Ignatieff rejects the assumptions in this argument, reasoning instead that "neither coercive interrogation nor torture is necessary, since entirely lawful interrogation can secure just as effective results." Ultimately, Ignatieff holds that "We cannot torture…because of who we are," that is, because of the ethical and treaty obligations that bind us as a nation.

As far as religious sensitivity to detainees is concerned, most of the people detained by U.S. forces are Arab Muslim men, who have specific religious beliefs and cultural practices that ought to be respected. Awareness of the need to show respect of this type to detainee arose because of a widely publicized story about a guard trying to flush a Koran down the toilet at the Guantánamo prison facility. As it happened, on May 15, 2005, the story was retracted by the newsmagazine that ran it because of lack of verification.[38] One positive outcome of this story was that those responsible for the well-being of detainees at Guantánamo were instructed about measures to take to ensure respect for the religious beliefs and cultural practices of the detainees. The Department of Defense has taken specific steps to educate U.S. forces about appropriate accommodations.

> A loudspeaker at Guantanamo now signals the Muslim "call to prayer" five times a day, and detainees get 20 minutes of uninterrupted time to practice their faith.
>
> Staff members schedule detainee medical appointments, interrogations and other activities in accordance with the prayer call schedule. Strict measures in place throughout the facility ensure appropriate treatment of the Koran, the Muslim holy book.
>
> Army Brig. Gen. Jay Hood, commander of Joint Task Force Guantanamo, said the task force respects Muslim dietary practices, flying in food that meets strict Islamic certification requirements and serving only menu items permitted under Muslim law.[39]

DIFFERENT RULES, OR TRADITIONAL RULES, FOR THE WAR AGAINST TERROR

Since the war against terror is different from conventional wars, what relevance do the traditional rules of war have for this type of war? There are no rules for war between large groups except the rules contained in the just war tradition. In modern times it was decided that the just war criteria applied to conflicts in which one of the parties was a revolutionary force. At that time, the era of the American Revolution and the French Revolution, it was decided that those who fought against each other were required to observe the international rules governing war. A terrible thing happened when terrorists attacked nations such as the United States, and it is reasonable that the nation retaliates in order to punish those who harmed it and destroy al-Qaeda's ability to inflict harm in the future. Notwithstanding, those who fight against terrorists need to maintain their own integrity and can do this by observing the limits of the just war tradition, especially the Geneva Conventions as these apply to treatment of prisoners. The just war tradition declares limits about what we can do to our enemies. By observing these limits we preserve our honor. As Kyle Fedler said:

> Terrorism is defined as the direct and intentional killing of innocent people with the purpose of achieving some greater goal, usually from the government of the people killed. If we engage in terrorism to combat terrorism, then the terrorists have surely already won.[40]

RESPONSIBILITIES OF PHYSICIANS AND NURSES

Do medical and nursing professionals function differently in the context of the war on terrorism than they function in other situations of war? Addressing this type of general question, Robert Jay Lifton, M.D., wrote on July 29, 2005:

> There is increasing evidence that U.S. doctors, nurses, and medics have been complicit in torture and other ille-

gal procedures in Iraq, Afghanistan, and Guantanamo Bay....

We know that medical personnel have failed to report to higher authorities wounds that were clearly caused by torture and that they have neglected to take steps to interrupt this torture. In addition, they have turned over prisoners' medical records to interrogators who could use them to exploit the prisoners' weaknesses or vulnerabilities. We have not yet learned the extent of medical involvement in delaying and possibly falsifying the death certificates of prisoners who have been killed by torturers.[41]

Abuses such as those that were recounted by Dr. Lifton are totally at odds with medical and nursing ethics. It is the responsibility of such professionals to render appropriate care to all persons and to do no harm to anyone. The fact that physicians and nurses are in the employ of the United States does not make them wartime partisans who can carry out an offensive mission against an enemy whom they encounter as a patient. Even if there is a tendency to hysteria during times of war and danger, members of the medical and nursing professions should rise above those sentiments and act in a dispassionate and responsible manner toward whomever they care for, friend or foe.

SUPPORT FOR GOVERNMENT PROPAGANDA

The U.S. government uses propaganda in support of its undertakings. This propaganda may or may not coincide with the experience of troops on the ground. If there is a divergence between what propaganda states and what troops see and hear, what responsibility do individual members of the military have to correct the record? This is a difficult question to answer because it depends on the way individual soldiers see their jobs. If she thinks of herself as a person with a job to do and orders to follow and who leaves the big picture to the officials at Centcom, then she will not be inclined to make waves. If, however, the soldier sees himself as a particularly well-informed citizen who has an obligation to participate meaningfully in his nation's democratic form of government, then he might speak to the media in order to set the record straight and turn public opinion into a force that militates in opposition to the war effort. If he follows such a path, of course, he will be placing himself in a difficult position, as he will probably suffer reprisals.

ROLE OF THE MEDIA

The media plays a large role in the formulation of public opinion. Leaders rely on a united populace in order to prosecute any war effectively. In view of this fact, should the media support the administration in its war efforts, or should it report honestly on the war against terror as it sees progress or lack thereof? The work of the media is to tell the truth and report on the events of the war, day by day, as they unfold, as well as the underlying policies and issues that need to be disclosed and discussed. In addition, the media should serve an educational function by breaking down stereotypes about Arab Muslims, and it should encourage critical thinking about the war. While, in the short term, presenting facts and underlying ideas may undermine support for the war, in the long run, no administration that represents a democracy should portray an undertaking as complex as a war in terms that do not coincide with reality.

Conclusion

As we have seen in this chapter, fighting terrorism is a complex subject, whether it is approached tactically or theoretically. In analyzing the theoretical issue of whether or not the just war tradition provides us with an adequate framework for determining the ethical boundaries of military engagement with terrorists, we have reviewed issues that are specific to this kind of war. Both civilian leaders who take the decision to go to war and members of the armed forces on the ground who prosecute the war face challenging and, perhaps, insurmountable barriers as they engage in the war on terror. Not only is the nation in danger from terrorists, the nation's leaders and its troops also risk surrendering their integrity as they seek to protect the country. It seems that the best way to prevent an erosion of integrity is by squarely addressing the topics raised here and deciding to follow the morally correct course.

Questions for Discussion

1. Discuss at least three specific ideas that should be included in a definition of terrorism.
2. The U.S. government responded differently to the Oklahoma bombing and the events of 9/11. If the nation had not responded to 9/11 with the "war on terror," what other options could leaders have taken? Discuss the advantages of one course over another.
3. Did the U.S.-led invasion of Iraq, which commenced on March 19, 2003, constitute a last resort, and was there a just cause for declaring war? Discuss the reasons for your position.
4. Why should troops who capture terrorists and guard terrorist prisoners treat these people with respect, and in what does respectful treatment consist?
5. Congressman John Murtha (D, PA), a decorated Vietnam veteran and longtime member of Congress, said that if he were a young man today, he would not join the military to fight in Iraq. Evaluate the ethical aspects of Murtha's position.
6. In January 2006, President George W. Bush said, "Thirty thousand Iraqis, more or less, have died as a result of the initial incursion and the ongoing violence against Iraqis." Discuss this fact in the context of the principle of noncombatant immunity.
7. Is it morally justifiable to bomb a building in which three terrorists and eighteen civilians are staying? Why or why not?
8. Laws and traditions in the United States that protect prisoners are stricter than those of some other countries. Is

it ethically acceptable for the United States to send suspected terrorists to other nations so that these suspects can be interrogated aggressively? Why or why not?

9. The United States operates a prison facility for suspected terrorists at Guantánamo Bay, Cuba. Discuss the rights of detainees to be charged for offenses and standards to be observed at trials for alleged crimes.

10. List and discuss three steps that should be taken to show respect for religious beliefs and practices of foreign prisoners in military detention.

11. Explain whether or not the war against terror should be fought within the general framework of the just war tradition.

Case Study

John Miller is the principal of a junior high school. In this capacity, he is familiar with the leaders in his community, including media executives. Mr. Miller's brother Paul is a pilot who flies for a U.S. intelligence agency, and the two men share an apartment. For the past few days, since his last flight, Paul has been acting anxious and depressed. While watching a football game on television, John asks Paul if there is something bothering him. The men have had too many beers and, as a result, both are uninhibited. Paul tells John that his last mission was a hard one. He picked up the bodies of two suspected terrorists who had been sent to a Third World country for aggressive interrogation and who had not survived the ordeal. As instructed, he dumped the bodies in the middle of the ocean. He had transported the men to the destination a week earlier and he was distressed at what had happened to them.

John Miller knows that his brother violated orders when he told his tale, and he believes Paul will never tell anyone else this story.

1. Based on what you have read in this chapter, what do you think John Miller should do with the information he learned from his brother?

2. What moral evaluation of the rendition of the two suspected terrorists would you offer? What prompts this evaluation?
3. Should Paul Miller continue his employment as a pilot for
   the U.S. intelligence agency? Why or why not?

NOTES

INTRODUCTION

1. Suspected al-Qaeda terrorist acts:

1993 (Feb.): Bombing of World Trade Center (WTC); 6 people killed.

1993 (Oct.): Killing of U.S. soldiers in Somalia.

1996 (June): Truck bombing at Khobar Towers barracks in Dhahran, Saudi Arabia, killed 19 Americans.

1998 (Aug.): Bombing of U.S. embassies in East Africa; 224 killed, including 12 Americans.

1999 (Dec.): Plot to bomb millennium celebrations in Seattle foiled when customs agents arrest an Algerian smuggling explosives into the United States.

2000 (Oct.): Bombing of the USS *Cole* in port in Yemen; 17 U.S. sailors killed.

2001 (Sept.): Destruction of WTC; attack on Pentagon. Total dead 2,992.

2001 (Dec.): Man tried to detonate shoe bomb on flight from Paris to Miami.

2002 (April): Explosion at historic synagogue in Tunisia left 21 dead, including 14 German tourists.

2002 (May): Car exploded outside hotel in Karachi, Pakistan, killing 14, including 11 French citizens.

2002 (June): Bomb exploded outside American consulate in Karachi, Pakistan, killing 12.

2002 (Oct.): Boat crashed into oil tanker off Yemen coast, killing one.

2002 (Oct.): Nightclub bombings in Bali, Indonesia, killed 202, mostly Australian citizens.

2002 (Nov.): Suicide attack on a hotel in Mombasa, Kenya, killed 16.

2003 (May): Suicide bombers killed 34, including 8 Americans, at housing compounds for Westerners in Riyadh, Saudi Arabia.

2003 (May): Four bombs targeting Jewish, Spanish, and Belgian sites in Casablanca, Morocco, killed 33 people.

2003 (Aug.): Suicide car bomb killed 12, injured 150 at Marriott Hotel in Jakarta, Indonesia.

2003 (Nov.): Explosions rocked a Riyadh, Saudi Arabia housing compound, killing 17.

2003 (Nov.): Suicide car bombers simultaneously attacked two synagogues in Istanbul, Turkey, killing 25 and injuring hundreds.

2003 (Nov.): Truck bombs detonated at London bank and British consulate in Istanbul, Turkey, killing 26.

2004 (March): Ten terrorists' bombs exploded almost simultaneously during the morning rush hour in Madrid, Spain, killing 202 and injuring more than 1,400.

2004 (May): Terrorists attacked Saudi oil company offices in Khobar, Saudi Arabia, killing 22.

2004 (June): Terrorists kidnapped and executed American Paul Johnson Jr. in Riyadh, Saudi Arabia.

2004 (Sept.): Car bomb outside the Australian embassy in Jakarta, Indonesia, killed 9.

2004 (Dec.): Terrorists enter the U.S. consulate in Jiddah, Saudi Arabia, killing 9 (including 4 attackers).

2005 (July): Bombs explode on three trains and a bus in London, England, killing 52.

Concerning above, see Web site: http://www.infoplease.com/ipa/A0884893.html

2. The motivation of the nineteen terrorists who hijacked planes on 9/11 is not easily stated, but the consensus of most commentators is that the reasons for the plot were ideological and the hijackers were part of a small, radical Islamic group.

3. http://www.rockymountainnews.com/drmn/america_at_war/article/0,1299,DRMN_2116_2882220,00.html

4. http://www.freep.com/apps/pbcs.dll/article?AID=/20060704/NEWS07/607040341/1009

5. http://www.chicagotribune.com/news/nationworld/chi-0607010091jul01,1,176063,print.story?coll=chi-newsnationworld-hed

6. http://today.reuters.com/News/newsArticle.aspx?type=topNews&storyID=2006-01-22T070219Z_01_N21227771_RTRUKOC_0_US-IRAQ-ABUSE.xml

Notes

1. THE JUST WAR TRADITION

1. http://www.whitehouse.gov/news/releases/2003/03/20030317-7.html

2. http://www.whitehouse.gov/news/releases/2003/02/20030319-17.html

3. http://www.historyguy.com/normandy_links.html

4. http://www.latimes.com/news/nationworld/nation/la-na-military1jul01,1,3487588.story?coll=la-headlines-nation&track=cross promo

5. Larry May, Eric Rovie, and Steve Viner, eds., *The Morality of War* (Upper Saddle River, NJ: Pearson/Prentice Hall, 2005), 28.

6. http://www.ppu.org.uk/learn/infodocs/st_justwar.html

7. May et al., *Morality of War,* 15.

8. Eileen P. Flynn, *My Country Right or Wrong? Selective Conscientious Objection in the Nuclear Age* (Chicago: Loyola University Press, 1985), 41–42.

9. http://www.newadvent.org/cathen/15068a.htm

10. http://www.jimmyakin.org/2004/06/kindler_gentler_1.html

11. James Turner Johnson, *Just War Tradition and the Restraint of War* (Princeton, NJ: Princeton University Press, 1981), 128–29.

12. http://pewforum.org/just-war/

13. Johnson, *Just War Tradition,* 94.

14. Ibid., 98.

15. Ibid., 99.

16. Ibid., 174.

17. Ibid., 166.

18. Ibid., 187.

19. May et al., *Morality of War,* 77.

20. Ibid., 116.

21. Peter Paret, "The Genesis of *On War,*" 21; *On War,* 91, 92, 579–610, in Carl von Clausewitz, On War, ed. and trans. by Michael Howard and Peter Paret (Princeton, NJ: Princeton University Press, 1976). At http://www.airpower.au.af.mil/airchronicles/aureview/1980/may-jun/etzold.html

22. http://www.civilwarhome.com/liebercode.htm

23. Johnson, *Just War Tradition,* 62.

24. Ibid., 317.

25. Ibid., 62, as quoted in Leon Friedman, ed., *The Law of War,* vol. I (New York: Random House, 1972), 313–14.

26. http://deoxy.org/wc/wc-nurem.htm

27. http://www.un.org/Overview/rights.html

28. http://www.redcross.lv/en/conventions.htm

29. http://www.icrc.org/ihl.nsf/0/e160550475c4b133c12563cd 0051aa66?OpenDocument

30. http://www.unhchr.ch/html/menu3/b/93.htm

31. http://www.icrc.org/Web/Eng/siteeng0.nsf/iwpList163/ 3CDB6A2F3EAA0EFFC1256B66005B01B2

32. http://www.converge.org.nz/pma/arape.htm

33. Flynn, *My Country*, 58.

34. http://pewforum.org/just-war/

35. Ibid.

36. Flynn, *My Country*, 58.

37. http://pewforum.org/just-war/

38. Ibid.

39. Ibid.

40. Ibid.

41. Flynn, *My Country*, 58.

42. http://pewforum.org/just-war/

43. Flynn, *My Country*, 58.

44. May et al., *Morality of War*, 17.

45. Ibid., 36.

46. Ibid.

47. http://www.cs.indiana.edu/statecraft/warpow.html

48. http://news.neilrogers.com/news/articles/2005121604.html

2. GOOD SOLDIERS: THEIR CONSCIENCES AND THEIR ACTIONS

1. http://www.centcom.mil/CENTCOMNews/news_release. asp?News Release=20040545.txt

2. http://news.bbc.co.uk/1/hi/world/middle_east/3727289.stm

3. http://go.reuters.com/newsArticle.jhtml?type=topNews&story ID=9771302&src=rss/topNews

4. http://www.sjcite.info/abughraib.html

5. http://webpac.lib.spc.edu:2076/universe/document?_m= c53aee0cba110e9a34a9e5e663bb0789&_docnum=109&wchp= dGLzVzz-zSkVb&_md5=6328924ed4384905905062368e334442

6. http://guantanamobile.org/blog/archives/cat_abu_ghraib_ in_the_courts.html

7. http://webpac.lib.spc.edu:2076/universe/document?_m= 09e9303c4a22ee6ea44b6e2315d28b8a&_docnum=44&wchp= dGLzVzz-zSkVb&_md5=88036ff862855e26fe4efc4d027b7eac

8. Ibid.

9. Eileen P. Flynn, *My Country Right or Wrong? Selective Conscientious*

Notes

Objection in the Nuclear Age (Chicago: Loyola University Press, 1985), 23.

10. Eileen P. Flynn, *Why Believe: Foundations of Catholic Theology* (Wisconsin: Sheed & Ward, 2000), 195.

11. http://www.ewtn.com/library/THEOLOGY/FR94304.htm

12. Flynn, *My Country*, 18–19.

13. Larry May, Eric Rovie, and Steve Viner, eds., *The Morality of War* (Upper Saddle River, NJ: Pearson/Prentice Hall, 2005), 427.

14. Ibid., 19.

15. Ibid., 20.

16. Ibid., 20.

17. Martin Luther King Jr., "Letter from the Birmingham Jail," in Ibid., 20.

18. http://www.oz.net/~vvawai/sw/sw36/heroes-massacres.html

19. http://www.vcdh.virginia.edu/HIUS316/mbase/docs/mylai.html

20. Associated Press, "Army Pilot Who Saved Villagers Dies," *St. Petersburg Times,* January 7, 2006, 1, 7A.

21. Ibid.

22. Flynn, *My Country*, 58.

23. http://www.priestsforlife.org/magisterium/bernardingannon.html

24. There are eight recorded instances of use of chemical weapons in armed conflicts: by the Germans in World War I; by Spain against Morocco, 1925; by the Soviet Union against China, 1934; by Italy against Ethiopia, 1935–1936; by Japan against China, 1937–1945; by Egypt against Yemen, 1963–1967; by the United States against Vietnam during the armed conflict in Southeast Asia; by Iraq against the Kurds, 1988. See L. F. Haber, *The Poisonous Cloud* (Oxford, UK: Clarendon Press, 1986); Steven Rose, *Chemical and Biological Warfare* (Boston: Beacon, 1968); Seymour M. Hersh, *Chemical and Biological Warfare* (Indianapolis: Bobbs Merrill, 1968); Don Oberdorfer, "US Says Iraq Used Poison Gas on Kurds," *Washington Post,* September 9, 1988, 1.

25. An example of harm from biological weapons is the death of forty-two people who died in April 1979 in Sverdlovsk, Siberia, as a result of inhaling airborne anthrax spores that were accidentally released. "Anthrax is a bacillus that has a dormant (spore) phase, then an active phase, in which it multiplies rapidly in the body, giving off fatal toxins. The spores may enter the body through the skin, they may be breathed, or they may be ingested with food." Philip J. Hilts, "U.S. and Russian Researchers Tie Anthrax Deaths to Soviets," *New York Times,* March 15, 1993, A6; the person or persons responsible for causing injury and death

to U.S. citizens by sending anthrax through the mail in the autumn of 2001, following the events of 9/11, has not been identified.

26. Louis Henkin, et al., *Basic Documents Supplement to International Law: Cases and Materials* (St. Paul, MN: West, 1980), 445–46.

27. "Paris Conference Calls for Complete Ban on Chemical Weapons," *UN Chronicle,* June 1989, 58.

3. RULES OF ENGAGEMENT

1. http://www.answers.com/topic/rules-of-engagement

2. http://en.wikipedia.org/wiki/Rules_of_engagement

3. Scott D. Sagan, "Rules of Engagement," in Alexander L. George, ed., *Avoiding War: Problems of Crisis Management* (Boulder, CO: Westview Press, 1991), 444.

4. http://www.9-11commission.gov/hearings/hearing12/myers_statement.pdf

5. Editorial, "Rules of Engagement Needed in Iraq," *Austin American Statesman,* March 8, 2005, A10.

6. John F. Burns, "U.S. Checkpoints Raise Ire in Iraq," *New York Times,* March 7, 2005, 1A.

7. http://www.globalsecurity.org/military/ops/iraq_orbat_coalition.htm. "As of July 1, 2005, there were 26 non–U.S. military forces participating in the coalition and contributing to the ongoing stability operations throughout Iraq. These countries were: Albania, Armenia, Australia, Azerbaijan, Bosnia and Herzegovina, Bulgaria, Czech Republic, Denmark, El Salvador, Estonia, Georgia, Italy, Japan, Kazakhstan, South Korea, Latvia, Lithuania, Macedonia, Mongolia, Netherlands, Norway, Poland, Romania, Slovakia, United Kingdom, and Ukraine." As of June 21, 2006, the United Kingdom had 8,000 troops on the ground; South Korea had 3,200; Italy, 2,600; Georgia, 900; Poland, 900; Romania, 860; Japan, 600; Denmark, 530; Australia, 470; El Salvador, 380; and all others combined, 1,156. Emi Doi and Tim Johnson, KRT News Service, "Japan Announces Plan to Withdraw Troops from Iraq," *Star Ledger,* June 21, 2006, http://www.nj.com/news/ledger/index.ssf?/base/news-7/1150868283162770.xml&coll=1.

8. Thom Shanker, "New Guidelines Are Reducing Iraqi Civilian Deaths, Military Says," *New York Times,* June 22, 2006, A13.

9. http://www.globalsecurity.org/military/intro/ied.htm

10. http://webpac.lib.spc.edu:2076/universe/document?_m=2e5fc8f16623da3fc1d7a67d7cbe34d7&_docnum=33&wchp=dGLbVtz-zSkVA&_md5=808b36e572012b09febc9fcbecc8a656

11. Patrick Quinn, Associated Press, "Car Bombs Are Vehicle to Wreak Destruction," *Star Ledger,* June 24, 2005, 17.

12. http://web.amnesty.org/library/Index/ENGMDE140712003? open&of=ENG-2M4

13. http://www.newsmax.com/archives/articles/2005/3/4/ 150408.shtml

14. http://nucnews.net/nucnews/2002nn/0204nn/020419nn. htm #325

15. http://www.washingtonpost.com/wp-dyn/articles/A52359-2004Nov15.html

16. http://www.centcom.mil/CENTCOMNews/News_Release. asp?NewsRelease=200305109.txt

17. http://webpac.lib.spc.edu:2076/universe/document?_m= f85f412696006c7cade300a0d51f3031&_docnum=25&wchp= dGLbVlb-zSkVA&_md5=724c228f465a39c709d1d6c51265d0f1

18. http://en.wikipedia.org/wiki/Afghanistan_friendly_fire_ incident#Findings_of_Board_of_Inquiry

19. Leon Friedman, ed., *The Law of War,* vol. I (New York: Random House, 1972), 4.

20. http://webpac.lib.spc.edu:2076/universe/document?_m= 2ac99d9b9121d9e6ca6c89f04664a22c&_docnum=15&wchp= dGLbVtz-zSkVA&_md5=189578b4061febc80bcec4f448f50df0

21. http://www.cbsnews.com/stories/2006/06/01/iraq/main167 3122.shtml

22. http://www.cbsnews.com/stories/2006/06/17/iraq/main17 26448.shtml

23. Alicia A. Caldwell, "Soldiers: We Were Under Orders to Kill," *Star Ledger,* July 22, 2006, 3.

24. Sagan, "Rules of Engagement," 462.

25. http://www.globalsecurity.org/military/library/report/1997/ Hall.htm

4. FIGHTING THE WAR ON TERROR WHILE HONORING THE JUST WAR TRADITION

1. http://www.cia.gov/terrorism/faqs.html

2. http://en.wikipedia.org/wiki/1993

3. http://www.okcbombing.org/

4. http://www.reference.com/browse/wiki/2001_anthrax_attacks

5. http://www.usdoj.gov/opa/pr/Pre_96/February95/78.txt.html

6. http://www.ict.org.il/spotlight/det.cfm?id=5

7. http://abcnews.go.com/US/wireStory?id=1525590

8. http://www.answers.com/topic/beltway-sniper-attacks

9. http://en.wikipedia.org/wiki/John_Allen_Muhammad

10. http://www.usatoday.com/news/nation/2004-03-10-malvo_x.htm

11. http://www.sptimes.com/News/111001/Worldandnation/FBI_Loner_in_US_sent.shtml

12. http://www.washingtonpost.com/wp-dyn/articles/A42754-2002Jan26_2.html

13. http://www.whitehouse.gov/news/releases/2002/01/20020129-11.html

14. http://www.answers.com/topic/george-w-bush

15. http://www.ips-dc.org/iraq/quagmire/

16. http://www.mtholyoke.edu/acad/intrel/bush/ultimatum.htm

17. http://cceia.org/viewMedia.php/prmID/5024

18. http://www.cbsnews.com/stories/2006/01/06/politics/main1182997.shtml

19. http://www.mtholyoke.edu/acad/intrel/bush/ultimatum.htm

20. http://sfgate.com/cgi-bin/article.cgi?f=/c/a/2005/12/13/MNG50G76G31.DTL

21. http://www.washingtonpost.com/wp-dyn/content/article/2006/06/08/AR2006060800152.html

22. http://www.brookings.edu/fp/saban/iraq/index20051121.pdf

23. Tim Golden, "A Junior Aide Had a Big Role in Terror Policy," *New York Times*, December 23, 2005, 1, A20.

24. http://www.pbs.org/newshour/bb/terrorism/july-dec05/debate_12-7.html

25. http://www.nytimes.com/2006/07/02/weekinreview/02liptak.html?pagewanted=1&ei=5087%0A&en=f80fae379386c6ba&ex=1151899200

26. http://en.wikipedia.org/wiki/Mujahid

27. http://www.washingtonpost.com/wp-dyn/content/article/2005/06/07/AR2005060700296.html

28. http://www.zogby.com/news/ReadNews.dbm?ID=1056

29. http://www.voanews.com/english/2006-01-22-voa27.cfm

30. http://www.timesofoman.com/newsdetails.asp?newsid=24466

31. http://www.newyorker.com/fact/content/?050214fa_fact6

32. http://usinfo.state.gov/xarchives/display.html?p=washfile-english&y=2005&m=July&x=20050720174600adynned0.488476&t=livefeeds/wf-latest.html

33. http://en.wikipedia.org/wiki/Guantanamo_Bay#Legal_status

Notes

34. http://webpac.lib.spc.edu:2076/universe/document?_m=30fc50693720356c037733ea385dcf2c&_docnum=50&wchp=dGLbVtz-zSkVb&_md5=e56f3884ba364ee5db0b9ea8053a6dc3

35. http://www.voltairenet.org/article133804.html

36. http://www.boston.com/news/nation/washington/articles/2006/01/04/bush_could_bypass_new_torture_ban/

37. http://www.prospect-magazine.co.uk/article_details.php?id=7374

38. http://www.cnn.com/2005/WORLD/asiapcf/05/15/newsweek.quran/index.html/

39. http://www.dod.gov/news/Jun2005/20050629_1904.html

40. http://www.crosscurrents.org/Felder.htm

41. http://www.wagingpeace.org/articles/2004/07/29_lifton_doctors-torture.htm

SELECTED BIBLIOGRAPHY

Albright, Madeleine. *The Mighty and the Almighty: Reflections on America, God, and World Affairs.* New York: HarperCollins, 2006.

Christopher, Paul. *The Ethics of War and Peace: An Introduction to Legal and Moral Issues.* 3rd ed. Upper Saddle River, NJ: Prentice Hall, 2004.

Donovan, Aine. *Ethics for Military Leaders.* 2nd ed. Needham Heights, MA: Pearson Custom Publishing, 1999.

Elshtain, Jean Bethke. *Just War against Terror: The Burden of American Power in a Violent World.* New York: Basic Books, 2003.

Flynn, Eileen P. *My Country Right or Wrong? Selective Conscientious Objection in the Nuclear Age.* Chicago: Loyola University Press, 1985.

George, Alexander L. *Avoiding War: Problems of Crisis Management.* Boulder, CO: Westview Press, 1991.

Hoffman, R. Joseph, ed. *Just War and Jihad: Violence in Judaism, Christianity, and Islam.* Amherst, NY: Prometheus Books, 2006.

Ignatieff, Michael. *Virtual War: Kosovo and Beyond.* New York: Henry Holt, 2000.

Ignatieff, Michael. *The Warrior's Honor: Ethnic War and the Modern Conscience.* New York: Henry Holt, 1998.

Johnson, James Turner. *Just War Tradition and the Restraint of War.* Princeton, NJ: Princeton University Press, 1981.

Johnson, James Turner. *Morality and Contemporary Warfare.* New Haven, CT: Yale University Press, 1999.

Johnson, James Turner. *The War to Oust Saddam Hussein: Just War in the New Face of Conflict.* Lanham, MD: Rowman & Littlefield, 2005.

Kane, Brian M. *Just War and the Common Good: Jus Ad Bellum Principles in Twentieth Century Papal Thought.* San Francisco: Catholic Scholars Press, 1997.

May, Larry, Eric Rovie, and Steve Viner, eds. *The Morality of War.* Upper Saddle River, NJ: Pearson/Prentice Hall, 2005.

Ramsey, Paul. *The Just War: Force and Political Responsibility.* Updated ed. Lanham, MD: Rowman & Littlefield, 2002.

Rebel, W. Rick, and George R. Lucas, eds. *Case Studies in Military Ethics.* New York: Longman, 2005.

Selected Bibliography

U.S. Conference of Catholic Bishops. *The Challenge of Peace: God's Promise and Our Response.* Mahwah, NJ: Paulist Press, 1983.

Walzer, Michael. *Arguing about War.* New Haven, CT: Yale University Press, 2004.

Walzer, Michael. *Just and Unjust Wars: A Moral Argument with Historical Illustrations.* 3rd ed. New York: Basic Books, 2000.

INDEX

Index

Index